12/3/63 (263-10 306)

Our Debt to Greece and Rome

EDITORS

GEORGE DEPUE HADZSITS, PH.D.

DAVID MOORE ROBINSON, PH.D., LL.D.

DEMOSTHENES
AND HIS INFLUENCE

BY

CHARLES DARWIN ADAMS, Ph.D.

COOPER SQUARE PUBLISHERS, INC.
NEW YORK
1963

Published 1963 by Cooper Square Publishers, Inc.
59 Fourth Avenue, New York 3, N. Y.
Library of Congress Catalog Card No. 63-10306

PRINTED IN THE UNITED STATES OF AMERICA

CONTENTS

[v]

DEMOSTHENES
AND HIS INFLUENCE

DEMOSTHENES
AND HIS INFLUENCE

I. THE LIFE OF DEMOSTHENES

FOR two reasons Demosthenes the Athenian holds a permanent place in the history of European civilization: first, as a statesman and practical politician he led the desperate struggle of the Athenian people to maintain the freedom of all the Greek city-states against the tide of imperialism which was sweeping down upon them from the North, and to defend the democracy of Athens from the extinction threatened by the Macedonian monarchy; second, Demosthenes was the first to embody completely the theories, devices, and embellishments of the new art of rhetoric in practical popular oratory. The preservation of Athenian liberty and democracy became the passion of his mature life; the perfected oratory of a generation which saw the flowering of

[3]

that noble art was his instrument. At a time when the art of public speech was in danger of becoming the mere plaything of literary display, or the cheap tool of ambitious demagogues, the fiery patriotism of Demosthenes lifted it to an eminence which gives to Greek oratory a place among the noblest products of the Greek genius.

For our knowledge of the personal life of Demosthenes we depend chiefly upon his own speeches and those of his contemporaries. The works of the contemporary historians are lost, and the surviving biographies of Demosthenes are late and unreliable, but we can recover the main course of events. We know that his father died when Demosthenes and his sister were little children, and that the executors of the estate embezzled much of the large property. Yet the mother was able to give the boy a good education, and in his late 'teens to provide for his instruction in rhetoric, and for his study of law under the ablest probate lawyer of the day, Isaeus. Demosthenes was a weakly youth, and the biographers agree in the story of his physical handicaps — his stammering utterance, his short breath, his awkward movements; and we have tales of mingled fact and fiction as to his persistent efforts to overcome these defects. As he came into manhood his first effort was to recover something of the family estate by prosecution of the executors. How far he succeeded we do not know, but we have the speeches in which he attacked them. Soon he entered upon the profession of speech-writing for the courts.

Under the Athenian system the parties to a suit were required to plead in person, though by consent of the jury each might call in friends to supplement his own plea. So there had grown up a profession which was prepared to furnish to the common citizen a speech which should cover the legal points of his case, and bring the art of rhetoric to the persuasion of the jury — in Athens always a large body, 200 to 500 in number, sometimes even more. A few of Demosthenes' speeches written to be delivered by clients have come down to us, some dealing with private affairs, others with public questions. We find in these speeches a rapidly developing skill in the years between his attaining his majority and his middle life, when he became exclusively occupied with politics. The speeches show a comprehensive knowledge of civil law and legal procedure; for the most part, clearness of statement, keenness in the discovery and arrangement of argument, effective use of the argument from probability where proof is lacking, vigor and sharpness in attack, and sometimes telling appeal to the sense of justice.

During Demosthenes' earlier professional years he was also giving instruction in rhetoric, though probably to only a small circle of friends, and with no thought of making this a profession. Very soon his ambition was turned toward a very different field of oratory, that of leadership in the popular assembly, the ecclesia. The immense powers of this popular body and the certainty with which a speaker who had their confidence and possessed the ability to move them by his oratory could influence public affairs, had led to the development of a distinct profession. These popular orators (ῥήτορες) ranged from venal demagogues to statesmen of the highest patriotism, who, following the example of Pericles, gave their lives to the State, serving quite as effectively by their influence from the bema as they could have done by any possible holding of office, though of course office-holding often accompanied their efforts as speakers before the

people. Naturally in those days as in our own
the ranks of the professional statesmen were
often filled from those of the lawyers. It was to
this career that Demosthenes turned after some
years of successful legal practice.

In order to appreciate the problems which
the Athenian state was facing in the middle of
the fourth century B.C. we must recall the significance of the system of Greek city-states
which had come down from the earliest times.
This system was wholly unlike the contemporary systems of Egypt or of Asia, and
equally strange as compared with the modern
conception of a 'State' as a body-politic occupying an extended territory with numerous
cities and towns, and perhaps ruling over remote lands and peoples. The Greek city-state
usually embraced but a single large town; out-
lying fields and villages extended only to some
near-by mountain barrier or river frontier; a
harbor town and a little stretch of coast-land
often completed the small domain, unless perhaps it had certain colonies in regions more or
less remote. Each of these little communities
was a sovereign state, making war and peace
with its neighbors, sending and receiving ambassadors, maintaining its army and navy, im-

posing its tariffs. Experience had, indeed, taught the necessity of making some modifications in this separative system. Again and again small groups of states had been forced into temporary union to repel the attack of some belligerent neighbor; once nearly all had been brought into alliance to push back the threatening Persian power. Certain attempts had been made to unite small groups of states without loss of local autonomy, and in some cases a powerful city had succeeded in extinguishing the independence of some of the small cities in its neighborhood, incorporating them wholly in its own territory; so both Sparta and Athens had done, and Thebes less successfully. But a more important form of union was that of the ' hegemony ' (leadership), a system in which a strong city, partly by offer of protection, too often by threat of aggression, sometimes by offer of trade privileges, persuaded a group of city-states to enter into treaty relation with herself, which bound them to follow her lead in war and to direct their interstate relations in harmony with her policies, while otherwise retaining their autonomy. The greatest experiment in hegemony had been that of Athens a century earlier in her Confederacy of Delos; but the fatal ambition of Pericles, transforming leadership into imperialism, had brought ultimate ruin. The next movement should have been toward federation, but the states were not yet ready for such surrender of local sovereignty and such an experiment in representative government. Toward the middle of the fourth century however there appeared to be good promise of a long period of quiet under the old system, with a fairly stable balance of power. Sparta had made her experiment in large imperialism after the Athenian failure, and she had failed as miserably. Sparta was no longer in position to menace any but her nearer and smaller neighbors. The strong Arcadian commonwealth, recently established by Epaminondas as a makeweight against Sparta, was a safeguard for the whole Peloponnesus. Thebes had enjoyed a meteoric career under the brilliant Epaminondas, but with his death she had fallen back to her old position, a strong but unprogressive state, satisfied now if she could control the small towns of her own Boeotia. Athens, fully recovered from the disasters of the Peloponnesian war, was at the head of a broad league of sea-states, held together by a constitution which guaranteed the members against abuses like those which had wrecked the Delian confederacy. She had a strong navy; her financial management was becoming wise and progressive; trade was flourishing; politics were in conservative hands; her people had given up their imperial ambitions; everything pointed to a new period of prosperity, involving Athenian leadership of the island states and many of those on the northern coasts, whose trade interests were served by connection with her. It is true that the Greek cities of the coast of Asia Minor were now hopelessly lost to the Greek world. Persia had easily re-established her control of them in the time when Athens and Sparta were engaged in their long struggle with each other. The Greek coast-cities were so closely connected with the Persian empire in their trade relations and so exposed to attack by land and sea that they had now neither hope nor desire for incorporation into the states of Greece; but there was no reason to fear any attempt of Persia to extend her power by sub-jugation of the island states.

And so when, in the year 360 B.C., Demos-thenes at the age of twenty-four was called out to serve as commander (trierarch) of a war vessel in an Athenian fleet operating in the

region of the Hellespont, he might well have
felt that the coming years were to be a time of
peace and increasing prosperity for all the
larger Greek states, and especially for Athens.
The operations in these northern waters were
intended to strengthen the relations of Athens
with the allies there; only one serious undertaking remained, the subjugation of Amphipolis, a once loyal Athenian colony, but long in
revolt. It certainly became clear to Demosthenes as the fleet cruised along these coasts
that the commercial prosperity of his city demanded such relations with the ports all along
the northern shores of the Aegean and the Hellespont clear to Byzantium, that her merchant
vessels would have secure passage to and from
the Black Sea ports — the source of an essential part of the Athenian grain supply, and important markets for her manufactures; it was
plain, too, that it was a wise policy by which
Athens was making colonial settlements on the
Chersonese. Such development need not, probably would not, involve any collision with the
old rivals of Athens. The program thus gradually shaping itself in the mind of Demosthenes
was entirely free from the old imperialism —
he never cherished any such illusion — but it

did involve the noble ambition to see his city the leader of the free sea-states, in secure possession of the freedom of the northern waters, and as of old the mother of prosperous colonies. Such a program was in accord with the best traditions of the past, and so far as one could see at this time it was entirely practicable.

But two years later (358) came news which showed the insecurity of such hopes. A group of the allied sea-states seceded from the Athenian confederacy. They no longer needed Athenian protection; some of them were tempted by the advantage of alliance with the Persian dependencies on the coast of Asia Minor, while Byzantium, the most important of the group, wished to resume her control of the straits, in order to regain the profitable tolls on traffic passing through. Athens attempted to bring the seceding states back by force, but after three years of costly effort she had to recognize their independence; her league was terribly crippled, her naval revenues cut down, and her prestige lowered.

Meanwhile the news had come of the succession of a young and vigorous king to the throne of Macedon. At first this gave no cause for alarm; the traditional relations between Athens and the royal house of Macedon had been friendly. The young king Philip made most friendly overtures, even undertaking to subdue for Athens the recalcitrant Amphipolis. Events followed with startling rapidity: Philip seized Amphipolis, but kept it in his own possession; he seized other coast towns; he allied himself with Olynthus, the most powerful city of the Chalcydic peninsula and the head of a strong federation there. News came of his organization of a powerful army on new and most efficient lines, and of his founding of a new city, Philippi, in the gold country of the river Strymon. He began ship building from the timber of the newly acquired territory; then he appeared with an army in Thessaly and gained foothold there by taking part in a dynastic struggle; returning to Thrace he rapidly extended his alliance along the great coast-road almost up to Byzantium. Finally an urgent call came to Athens from Olynthus; Philip had thrown off his alliance with them and his army was moving upon the city.

The Athenians had not been indifferent to the menacing progress of Philip in the north during these seven years. Upon his seizure of

Amphipolis they had determined to send troops
against him, but by this time the secession from
the naval confederacy was fully under way,
and the attempt to reduce the seceding allies
demanded all the powers of the state. A little
fleet with hired troops was all that could be
sent to the north, and it was miserably ineffec-
tive. It was at this time that Demosthenes began to take an active part in the debates in
the ecclesia. His personal knowledge of the
northern coasts and his appreciation of their
vital relation to Athenian commerce, as well
as his pride in the traditional sea-power of
Athens, impelled him to urge vigorous resistance to the new Macedonian power. He early
recognized Philip as a man who would not be
content with the mere restoration of Macedon
to its old local power. Demosthenes saw that
Philip had ambition and ability which would
threaten the peace of all northern Greece, and
he threw himself into the struggle to arouse
the Athenians to a realization of the gravity of
the situation. Some of his brief fiery harangues
have come down to us; in them he denounces
the indifference of the people, the unwillingness
of the rich to tax themselves to support the
fleet, and of the masses to serve in person; he

warns them that if Philip gains control of the North, there will be nothing to hinder his intervening in the troubled affairs in north-central Greece, and even moving upon Athens herself; he warns them of the irreconcilable hostility between an irresponsible monarchy and a free democracy; he recalls the glories of old Athens, and contrasts them with the present humiliation of the state; he denounces the politicians who have enriched themselves while they have let the city become impoverished; he calls on the people to cease draining the treasury by their foolish doles for the festivals; he urges them to restore the fleet and to decree universal military service.

Demosthenes' appeals were not altogether in vain, although he could not persuade the people that the crisis was in any way as desperate as he pictured it. War measures were voted, troops were enrolled, but unfortunately at the very time when help for Olynthus was demanded, a crisis had arisen very near home: an Athenian force on the island of Euboea had been betrayed and surrounded, and instant effort had to be made for its rescue. By the time this was accomplished, it was too late to send effective help to Olynthus; the city and

its allied Chalcydic towns were in the hands
of Philip.

At the same time the situation in north-
central Greece gave cause for anxiety on the
part of the Athenians. For eight years the
Amphictyonic league had been at war with
Phocis, the little state in which lay the shrine
of Apollo at Delphi. The Phocians had become
involved in a dispute with the Amphictyons,
and had seized Delphi, sacrilegiously appro-
priated the golden votive treasures of the temple, and with this gold were maintaining a formidable mercenary army. Thebes, moved quite
as much by political as religious considerations,
was taking the lead against them. Unable to
overcome the Phocian troops, the Thebans were
appealing now to Philip to come to the help of
the god — and of themselves. Should he accept
this invitation, he would obtain foothold in
central Greece, he would have all the prestige
of championship of the god of Delphi, and he
would have close alliance with Thebes. All this
would mean that Philip's power would reach to
the very borders of Attica. Under these circumstances it was with surprise and relief that
the Athenians received word — at first through
unofficial channels — that Philip would be glad

[16]

to make a treaty of peace with them. Demosthenes, by this time recognized as the leader of the anti-Macedonian group, was now at one with the conservatives, who had from the first deprecated the hostile attitude of the city toward Philip. All were agreed that every effort must now be made to negotiate an honorable peace. If this could be done it was hoped that the Macedonian power might be held within its present limits — a power formidable indeed, but still restricted to the North Country. Commissions passed back and forth, a treaty of peace and alliance was formulated, and after considerable delay, was signed by Athens and the members of her confederacy and by Philip and his allies. Demosthenes was a leader in all the negotiations, and a member of the two embassies which went to Macedonia to negotiate and ratify the treaty. But in the final negotiations Demosthenes' suspicion and fear were thoroughly aroused. He knew that an essential item in the peace treaty would be a provision to prevent Philip's intervention in the Phocian war. But all his efforts to provide for this in the treaty by the inclusion of the Phocian state as allied with Athens were in vain. Demosthenes became convinced that certain members of the Athenian embassy had gone over into the pay of Philip, and on their return to Athens he denounced them, and declared his fear that under cover of the peace Philip was preparing to intervene against the Phocians. Almost immediately his fears were proved to be justified. Philip, marching down through Thermopylae, expelled the Phocian mercenary army, wiped out the fortified towns of the district, and confirmed the friendship of Thebes, not only by helping her to bring to an end the long and vexatious war, but also by restoring to her control the long-recalcitrant smaller Boeotian cities. Philip himself now stood forth as the arbiter of affairs in all north-central Greece. He was promptly received into the Amphictyonic Council and became virtual dictator there. He could no longer be stigmatized as an outsider, a ' barbarian '; and in all these acts Philip had in no way violated his newly-made treaty with Athens.

There followed a period of restless activity on the part of Philip. He not only constantly used his now thoroughly trained and enthusiastic Macedonian veterans in military expeditions, but he developed a skill in diplomacy and an ability to win over and manipulate leading

citizens in other states which marked him as
the peer of any public man in Greek history.
He now thoroughly established his control of
the long coast-road eastward from Macedonia,
and with it the control of all the small harbors
along the coast, thus menacing the trade route
to and from Byzantium and the Black Sea.
At the same time he was enlarging his fleet;
while it was no match for that of Athens, it was
quite sufficient to endanger the Athenian merchant vessels on the grain route, if hostilities
should arise. In Thessaly he reorganized their
long-disturbed government, and had himself
elected Overlord of Thessaly for life. Passing
westward he established his wife's brother as
king of the Molossians, and threatened more
than one of the districts on the northwest coast.
In the Peloponnesus he established connection
with the states which were living in fear of
Spartan aggression, the Arcadians, Messenians,
and Argives, subsidizing their troops, and appearing to them in the guise of Liberator. Westward in Elis, rent by civil war, he made connection with the victorious faction, and so
became a patron of another sacred spot, Olym-
pia. In Euboea, just across the narrow strait
from Attica, troops sent by Philip helped local

tyrants to win control in two of the important towns. In Megara, the key to the Isthmus of Corinth, partisans of Philip made a similar attempt with the aid of mercenary forces sent by him, but were thwarted by Athenian troops.

As the news of all these operations, military and diplomatic, came to Athens in quick succession, the people began to realize that Philip was drawing his net tight around Attica; and it was most exasperating to be forced to admit that in doing all this Philip was in no slightest degree violating the terms of the peace. They had hoped to tie his hands by the treaty; they realized now that they had only tied their own. No state which was now suffering his aggressions had been included in the treaty, no item of his agreement with them was violated; and yet his whole course threatened to be fatal to their continued influence among the states of Hellas, and even to their own independence. Philip would very soon be in a position to lay down his own terms to them; they would exist as a State only by his sufferance.

In the five years in which Philip's power had been thus developing under cover of the Peace, Demosthenes had been confirmed in his conviction that there could be no permanent peace between Athens and Philip. Perhaps in the early stages of the negotiations for peace Demosthenes had hoped that his earlier fears of Philip might prove unjustified; but now there was no question in his mind — Philip was aiming at nothing less than supremacy over all Hellas. Demosthenes now made it his one business to arouse the Athenians to a sense of their danger, to open the eyes of other states which were looking upon Philip as a benefactor, and to organize a confederacy which should be able to put a stop to the Macedonian advance. This involved an outright break with the conservative leaders, Phocion and Eubulus, men of the highest character, with whom until recently he had coöperated.

It is just here, in the five years following the peace treaty of 346, that we must form our judgment of the statesmanship of Demosthenes. His earlier efforts to check the aggressions of Philip on the northern coasts were unquestionably justified. But now, with the Macedonian power fully developed, with its relation to Athens defined by a treaty of peace and alliance, the terms of which were being scrupulously observed by Philip, was it wise to denounce the peace, to embitter the Athenians against Philip, and to lead them into a perilous war, the issues of which must be so momentous? First, was the policy practicable? Was not the power of Philip now so great that war against him was foolhardy? He had a veteran army, a staff of generals any one of whom was superior to any man in any other Greek state, he had under him the famous Thessalian cavalry, and his supplies of gold for employing mercenary troops were abundant; above all, he was himself a military genius of the first rank. Was it not suicidal for peace-loving Athens, a state whose military power had always been chiefly naval, to bring on a war in which her raw militia, poorly led, must meet the armies of Philip in the field? Demosthenes' policy was certainly a daring one, but it seemed to him that success was more than possible. The very fact that the Macedonian power was now over-shadowing all Greece might be expected to alarm other Greek states and unite them with Athens. Much depended on Thebes; she had put herself under obligation to Philip, and his representatives were strong there, but now that Philip was in complete control of her neighbors on the north, she might well question her own security; she was jealous of Athens, but she had nothing to fear from her; it might well be that Thebes could be persuaded to lend her formidable strength to an anti-Macedonian movement. Other states, if less powerful than Thebes, might each contribute men and money to a war of self-defence, if a state like Athens would take the lead. And there was a growing hope that the Persian King would soon realize that if Philip gained control of all Greece his ambition would carry him across the Helles-pont into the rich provinces of Persia, and that perhaps in the end he might organize an expe-dition into the heart of the Persian empire, a rich field, now notoriously ripe for plunder. The aged Athenian Isocrates was already in an open letter urging Philip to undertake such an expedition; it was his next logical step. Ordi-nary prudence would suggest to the Persian administrators on the coast to urge upon the King the giving of such abundant subsidies to an anti-Macedonian movement in Greece as to enable its leaders to gather together enough professional mercenary troops — in these days very abundant on both sides of the Aegean — to be more than a match for the armies of Philip. Demosthenes was working for just this help. With the Athenian navy in command of the sea, and Thebes barring the way into central Greece, it might be hoped that the war would be fought in Macedonian territory. It may seem to some a strange and disappointing thing that Demosthenes should invite the help of the hereditary enemy, Persia — it certainly gave his political enemies an opening of which they joyously availed themselves, ' Demosthenes trafficking in Persian gold.' But it would not be the first instance of such a policy. When Athens lay prostrate after the Peloponnesian war, it was Persian help that lifted her up and rebuilt her walls. Hereditary enmities have a way of disappearing in national emergencies. These words are written near the old Indian trail along which year after year French officers led down bands of savages from Canada to ravage the English settlements in the lower Connecticut valley. But when, hardly a generation later, the New Englanders were in desperate war against their mother country, they welcomed with open arms the French troops who came to their rescue. We ourselves have seen centuries of enmity between England and France forgotten in the face of the German peril. He must be blind both to the facts of history and the events of his own time who can reproach Demosthenes for seeking subsidies from Persia to help defend the free Greek states against the Macedonian Lord and Master. But our question is: Was all this plan of war so far practicable as to give reasonable hope of success, and to warrant the view on our part that Demosthenes was a man of practical judgment, and not a blind fanatic? The considerations which have been presented would seem to justify his belief that Athens had more than a ' fighting chance,' and to warrant his insistent plea that Athens take her place as leader of a war of defence against the new power in the north.

But a more important question is this: Was it not a mistake for Athens to refuse to place herself under the hegemony of Philip? There is every reason to believe that had she ceased her opposition to him, he would have treated her generously; she would have become a member of a united Hellenic league under the efficient leadership of Philip. She would have sacrificed only her freedom of action in inter-state affairs. Autonomous, prosperous in trade, probably sharing in a career of Asiatic conquest, freed from the never-ending wars of petty Greek states, would not Athens have been

[25]

happier and more prosperous under Macedonian hegemony? To answer that question the modern reader must put himself into the environment of an Athenian of the time of Demosthenes; he must remember that from the earliest times it had been the pride of Athens always to lead — never to follow; she had early learned to command, she had never learned to obey. Again and again Athens had stood forth as Liberator; not only had she been foremost champion in the wars against Persia, but many a time she had protected the weaker state against the stronger. To resign all this, to become a single unit on the outskirts of a Macedonian league, would be to break with all the traditions of her past. To a man who, like Demosthenes, had gone to Thucydides for his political ideals this was unthinkable. Doubtless had England and all Europe at the opening of the twentieth century been willing to enroll themselves in a league under the absolute dictation of a Kaiser, it would for a time have been conducive to the peace of Europe, countless lives would have been saved, trade and manufacture would have flourished mightily. But we can hardly reproach an English statesman for not advocating such a policy for 'Old Eng-

land.' And ' Old Athens' had her traditions and
her pride. She too knew what it was to be mistress of the sea; and Demosthenes was an
Athenian.

But we are told nowadays that while we
may admire Demosthenes as a loyal Athenian
and justify his policy from the purely Athenian
standpoint, we cannot credit him with the
larger vision and with supreme statesmanship;
for the time had come, we are told, when even
an Athenian statesman ought to have seen that
the old system of petty city-states must give
way to a union of Hellas; experience had
proved the old system to be a miserable failure;
and now, under the lead of a man of marvelous
organizing ability, the opportunity was offered
of uniting the little Greek states once for all;
it was their God-given opportunity; it is lam-
entable that Demosthenes had not vision
enough to look beyond the local pride of his
own little state and see the possible salvation of
all Hellas. Such was the judgment of students
of Greek history who in the early years of the
twentieth century were sharing in the splendid prosperity of a Germany which had been
forced to give up its petty separative system of
independent states, and had come forth as a

mighty world-power under the lead of a fighting kingdom and a military dynasty — a kingdom and a dynasty which were in many ways a modern repetition of the Macedonian. Why could not Demosthenes have seen the possibilities which lay in union under Macedon!

Now they are right who say that union of the Greek states was the need of the hour, and a broader and firmer union than any of the past hegemonies. Even forced union under a monarchical state might have been desirable, if the monarch had been a representative of the best Greek traditions and a man whose ambition was the development of all Hellas in the ways of peace, and provided, too, the ruling state was representative of the best civilization of the Greeks, so that the character of her supremacy would not depend on the life of a single man. But union under Macedon and its ruling house had in it no such promise. Philip's ambitions were those of conquest, never of peace, and his whole conception of government was that of the irresponsible monarch; the day of Philip's supremacy in any state marked the end of free government there; the name of freedom might remain, but the substance was gone — Philip's personal agents were hence-

forth the rulers. And the Macedonian people
as a whole were still in the predatory stage of
civilization; war would be the chief concern
of any union of states under Macedon. Such a
dynasty and such a ruling people could hold
the Greek states together only by force, and
only at the cost of all that makes civic life
precious. But we are not dependent on theories
for our judgment of the effect on Hellas of a
union under Philip. The union was in fact
completely effected, despite the opposition of
Demosthenes and the Athenians. After 338
practically all of Hellas was subject to the dictation of Philip; upon his assassination two years
later the consolidated power passed to his brilliant son Alexander. The new king led his
Greek armies to the conquest of Asia, and the
glorious success of a united Hellas seemed on
the point of realization. Then came the catas-
trophe. On the death of Alexander his kingdom fell apart; his generals divided his realm,
and from that time on they and their successors
ceaselessly warred with one another in their
ambitious rivalries and personal enmities; national considerations no longer counted; personal ambitions and dynastic enrichment were
the prizes in a ceaseless war-game in which the

[29]

little states of Greece were insignificant pawns. Their free governments were at an end. Now they were rising in revolt against an oppressive government, now fawning on some princely liberator and benefactor; allying themselves now with one empire — Ptolemaic, Seleucid — now with another; never secure, never free. Those who argue that under Philip the opportunity of a united Hellas was offered and should have been accepted, might well read the story of the actual union as told in Ferguson's *Hellenistic Athens*. Writing of Athens in the period of forty-six years from 307 B.C. (fifteen years after the death of Demosthenes) to 261 B.C., Ferguson says: " Seven times the government changed hands, and on as many occasions the constitution was in some degree altered. Three different parties with different ideals and traditions strove for the mastery, and as often as a change came, the foreign policy of Athens was reversed. Four times the institutions were modified and a new government established through the violent intervention of a foreign prince. Three uprisings were bloodily suppressed, and the city sustained four blockades, all with equal heroism, but twice unsuccessfully. Athens was rarely the instigator of trouble in this long period of disaster, but she seldom escaped being drawn into the struggle which others had precipitated." It was in this period that the Macedonian king Demetrius did Athens the honor of graciously accepting her fawning flatteries and deification, finally for one winter making the Parthenon itself the banquet-hall and the bed-chamber of himself and the notorious courtesan Lamia — one generation after the warnings of Demosthenes. If Demosthenes had any failure of vision it was a failure to see the depths of ruin to which Macedonian supremacy was to plunge the free states of Hellas. True, its conquests carried Greek culture to the whole Eastern world and planted splendid Greek cities in Asia and Africa, but it killed the free institutions of Greece itself, and it dried up forever the springs of her artistic and literary genius. Something of this civic disaster Demosthenes in his time did foresee, and he threw all the power of his life into the struggle to save Athens, and with her the other Greek states. The justification of the struggle even in the face of her utter defeat in the field we read in Demosthenes' own words: " Had the future been foreseen by all, had all foreknown, and had you, Aeschines, warned and protested with shouts and cries, — you who did not open your mouth — even so the city could not have held back from this course, if she had any regard for glory, or for her fathers or her future honor. . . . Had she yielded up without a struggle those things for which our fathers underwent every danger, who would not have spit upon — YOU, not upon the city nor upon me. With what face, by heaven, could we have looked into the eyes of men visiting our city, if events had turned out as they now have, and Philip had been chosen leader and lord of all, but the struggle to prevent it had been made by other men, apart from us! Never in former days has our city chosen inglorious safety in place of danger in behalf of honor. . . . Never in all time has any man been able to persuade Athens to attach herself to the strong but unjust, and so enjoy safe slavery; but rather she has continued to struggle for leadership and honor and glory, ALWAYS."[1] (*De Cor.*, 199 ff.)

And so in the five years which followed the making of the Peace of Philocrates, Demosthenes threw himself completely into the attempt to arouse the Athenians to a sense of the

danger which threatened them in the swiftly
advancing power of Philip, and to warn other
states of the insidious Macedonian propaganda
which was corrupting leading citizens among
them and making them the secret agents of
Philip. At first Demosthenes seemed a blatant
agitator, in time of peace now denouncing and
misrepresenting a king who was scrupulously
living up to the letter of his agreement, now
viciously attacking fellow-citizens who stood
for peace and friendly relations with Macedon.
But as more and more the designs of Philip
became manifest, Demosthenes' speeches took
on a tone of the highest statesmanship. The
two speeches which belong to the close of this
period, the speech *On Affairs in the Chersonese*
and the *Third Philippic*, are masterpieces of
honest, wise, and impassioned pleading. Gradually Demosthenes succeeded in winning the
majority of the people to his view of the danger from Macedon. His missions far and wide
among the Greek states resulted in the forma-
tion of an anti-Macedonian alliance with very
considerable resources. At last, at the very
crisis, he won over Thebes herself, the key
to the strategic situation.

The open break came on the northern coasts

through petty collisions of Athenian troops and ships with those of Philip. The first trial of strength was at Byzantium. That city had become alarmed at Philip's steady eastward advance and had withdrawn from alliance with him. An Athenian fleet went to her rescue as she lay under siege by Philip, and he was forced to withdraw. The situation was promising, as Philip led his troops away into the northern districts. Then came a wholly unexpected disaster: another miserable, little Amphictyonic war broke out in north central Greece; before it could be settled Philip with his full military force was on the ground, safe below Thermopylae, the champion of the Delphic god, as he had every right to be. But the real campaign, as was evident to everyone from the first moment, was against Athens and her allies. The battle of Chaeronea in 338 was a defeat for the allies so overwhelming that there was no possibility of further resistance. Philip's terms to Athens were unexpectedly moderate, but they involved the dissolution of her confederacy and the complete recognition of Macedonian hegemony, under which a synod of the Greek states was established, to meet regularly at Corinth. From this time on the organization

of the army for the invasion of the Persian
kingdom absorbed the attention of Philip, and
then of his son and successor, Alexander.

Even the overwhelming defeat at Chaeronea,
with the loss of a thousand Athenians killed
and two thousand taken prisoners, did not
shake the confidence of the people in the
leadership of Demosthenes. He was chosen to
deliver the eulogy of those who had fallen in
the war, and repeated attacks by his personal
and political enemies were defeated in the
courts by the good-will of the Athenian jurors.
Although the political leadership inevitably
passed to men who were in favor with Philip,
Demosthenes still held the confidence and love
of the people. Nor did he despair of the cause
of Greek liberty; he worked steadily with
others of his party in providing for the repair
of the fortifications, and in otherwise putting
the city into condition to seize any opportunity
which the future might offer. Most important
were his continued negotiations with Persia for
subsidies for the anti-Macedonian movement.
It was matter of common knowledge that Philip
was preparing to cross the Hellespont and in-
vade the maritime provinces of Persia. Demosthenes now began to receive considerable sums

of Persian gold to be used in furthering movements which should keep Philip occupied in Greece. This was most dangerous business for Demosthenes; in the nature of the case it had to be kept secret so far as possible, and it offered occasion for all manner of suspicion of his personal motives and conduct; but he was courageous enough to do the dangerous thing. The assassination of Philip and the accession of the young and unknown Alexander, two years after Chaeronea, gave sudden hope to the anti-Macedonian party throughout Greece. Demosthenes was instantly active in urging revolt, but fortunately Athens delayed open action. Thebes, more prompt in following the policies of Demosthenes, was overwhelmed by the sudden descent of the young king; her annihilation — the bare ground where the great city had stood left as the witness of the Macedonian power and wrath — warned Athens and the rest of Hellas that the new master of Greece would brook no opposition. Demosthenes and the other patriot leaders had been deeply compromised in the preparations for revolt, and it was only with difficulty that Alexander was persuaded by Athenian friends of Macedon to withdraw his demand for their surrender. Having quieted Greece by his prompt measures, Alexander proceeded to the invasion of Asia; as news came year after year of his marvelous conquests, hope of resistance to his overlordship died in the hearts of all but the most fanatical patriots. Demosthenes was too wise a man to continue the hopeless struggle. The extremists of his party began to accuse him of having gone over to Macedon!

Two years after the battle of Chaeronea, Ctesiphon, a friend of Demosthenes, wishing to give public expression to the continued confidence of the people in the leader who was sharing with them their sorrow over the lost cause, had moved a decree by which a golden wreath should be awarded Demosthenes in the great theatre at the coming festival of Dionysus, with a resolution of the popular assembly testifying to his unwearied services to his country. The proposed decree was attacked as illegal by Aeschines, the most bitter enemy of Demosthenes, and an orator second only to him in ability. Seven years before, Demosthenes had prosecuted Aeschines in the courts on the charge of treason in the peace-embassy. While he had not secured conviction, he had discredited Aeschines with the people, and left him under the suspicion (probably entirely unwarranted) of being a paid agent of Philip. Aeschines now saw the opportunity for revenge. The attack of Aeschines carried the proposal for crowning to the law court, where not only its technical legality, but, by the looseness of the Athenian legal procedure, the merits of the proposal itself would be argued and decided. The trial of the case was delayed for reasons unknown to us, but six years later, in 330, Ctesiphon and his motion came to trial. Aeschines' speech in prosecution and that of Demosthenes in defence of Ctesiphon are the two famous speeches *On the Crown*.

In certain technical particulars the proposed crowning violated clear provisions of the laws — matters of time and place. Aeschines made a convincing argument on these points, but he himself declared that his own interest was chiefly in proving Demosthenes unworthy of the honor at any time and in any place. He reviewed Demosthenes' whole career, picturing the disastrous results of his policies, and stigmatizing him as the child of ill-fortune, the object of the wrath of the gods; a man who ruined every person and every cause that he touched. With dramatic effect Aeschines pic-

tures the ruin of Thebes and the disasters of
Athens as the result of Demosthenes' leadership. What words can the herald utter as he
proclaims the decree before the assembled
multitudes in the theatre? " If he shall recite
the mere dictates of the decree, yet the truth,
ashamed, will refuse to be silent, and we shall
seem to hear her crying out in words which con-
tradict the voice of the herald, ' This man,'
if man he can be called, ' the Athenian people
crown,' the basest — ' for his virtue! and for
his nobility ' — the coward and deserter! No!
by Zeus and the gods, do not, my fellow citizens, do not, I beseech you, set up in the
orchestra of Dionysus a memorial of your own
defeat; do not in the presence of the Greeks
convict the Athenian people of having lost their
reason; do not remind the poor Thebans of
their incurable and irreparable disasters —
men who, exiled through Demosthenes' acts,
found refuge with you, when their shrines and
children and tombs had been destroyed by Demosthenes' taking of bribes and by the Persian gold. But since you were not present in
person, yet in imagination behold their disaster; imagine that you see their city taken, the
razing of their walls, the burning of their

homes; their women and children led into captivity; their old men, their aged matrons, late in life learning to forget what freedom means; weeping, supplicating you, angry not so much at those who are taking vengeance upon them, as at the men who are responsible for it all; and calling upon you by no means to crown the curse of Hellas, but rather to guard yourselves against the evil genius and the fate that ever pursue the man. For there is no city, there is no private man — not one — that has ever come off safe from following Demosthenes' counsel." (§§ 155 ff.)

In reply Demosthenes made light of the charges as to time and place, waiving them aside with plausible quibbles, and gave his whole strength to the justification of his policy of opposition to Philip. Reviewing his public career step by step he shows that his policy was the only one possible for sons of the men of Marathon and Salamis, who saw Philip threatening the enslavement of Hellas. No choice was left to Athens; success in the field hung on the decree of Fortune; the honorable struggle for liberty was within their own power, and they had carried it through with a spirit worthy of the Athens of old.

Although at the time the Macedonian success in Asia was at its height and the subjugation of the Greek states was complete, the Athenian jury gave an overwhelming verdict to Demosthenes. Aeschines, defeated and humiliated, soon left the city and spent the rest of his life in voluntary exile.

The period which followed the trial of the Crown case was one of little political activity. Demosthenes coöperated with leaders of the other party in developing the internal resources of the city. It was no time for efforts against the Macedonian power, and a time of quiet was welcome to all parties. There was, however, one most unfortunate affair, which involved Demosthenes deeply, and in the eyes of many has cast a shadow on his reputation. Harpalus, a runaway viceroy of Alexander, who had been entrusted with large treasures of gold in Babylon, appeared in Greece, asking the Athenians to harbor him, and offering to put the gold at their disposal. The question was debated in the ecclesia, and finally, on motion of Demosthenes, Harpalus was put under arrest, and his treasure was ordered deposited in the Athenian treasury on the Acropolis, awaiting instructions from Alexander — the only honor-

[41]

able and safe course for the city to take. But shortly after, it was learned that only a part of the gold was in the treasury, and the escape of Harpalus himself soon followed. Charges and suspicion filled the air. Agents of Alexander demanded the gold. Investigation by the Areopagus followed. The outcome was the finding of indictments by the Areopagus against a group of public men, as having in one way or another received a part of the Harpalus treasure; the name of Demosthenes was on the list. The case went to the law courts, and Demosthenes was found guilty. Condemned to pay a fine of fifty talents, and unable to meet this demand, he escaped from prison and went into exile. With our incomplete knowledge of the facts, it is impossible to determine the merits of the case. So much of partisan feeling was involved and so many personal enmities, and the necessity of placating Alexander by finding some one guilty was so pressing, that the verdict of the Areopagus and of the court cannot be regarded as decisive. It is hard to believe that a man of Demosthenes' experience, publicly known to have made himself responsible for the arrest of Harpalus and the sequestration of his treasure, could have been so foolish as to pilfer the gold, or to receive bribes from the man. Some think he took the gold, but for use in the anti-Macedonian cause. The whole affair remains a notorious and mysterious scandal.[2]

In the summer of 323 the news of the sudden death of Alexander in Babylon reached Greece. A wide-spread movement to throw off the Macedonian control immediately followed. What had begun as a mere ' hegemony ' had already become outright imperialism, and states which had originally been content to accept Macedonian leadership were eager now to regain their freedom. The Athenians, against the advice of some of their ablest statesmen, voted extraordinary measures to equip a large fleet and to put almost the whole body of their militia into the field. Demosthenes, who was already furthering the movement while still in exile, was recalled — his fine remitted by a pious fiction — and he was welcomed back to the city with general acclaim. Leosthenes, the able Athenian general, led a large army into the north, past Thermopylae, into Thessaly, and with a large body of allies from northern Greece was at first successful against the army sent down from Macedonia. But the arrival of large bodies of Macedonian reinforcements and the death of Leosthenes turned the scale. In the battle of Crannon (August, 322) the Greek losses were so heavy that the alliance began at once to melt away, and the Athenian army was left supported only by the Aetolians. Nothing remained but to sue for peace. Antipater, the Macedonian regent, demanded unconditional surrender. His final peace terms were the return of Athens into the Macedonian alliance, the reception of a Macedonian garrison in her harbor fort, the payment of a heavy war indemnity, the restriction of the franchise by imposing a property qualification which would reduce the voters from 21,000 to 9,000, and the surrender of the public men who had instigated the revolt. The Athenians had no alternative. The terms were accepted, and the government passed into the hands of the pro-Macedonian leaders.

Demosthenes and the other proscribed patriots fled from the city, but were pursued by the agents of Antipater. The orator Hyperides and two others were arrested in a temple at Aegina; sent to Antipater, they were executed by his orders. Demosthenes had taken refuge on the near-by island Calauria. Discovered there by the posse of Antipater's soldiers sent out for his arrest, he remained in a temple-asylum long enough to take the poison which he carried with him, and only his lifeless body fell into the hands of the emissaries of the Macedonian.

The death of Demosthenes and of his associates in the anti-Macedonian party left Athens in the hands of men who were content to take their orders from the court of Macedon. The most successful popular leader henceforth was the man who could invent the most fulsome flatteries for the overlords, or persuade the people that by exchanging servitude to one dynasty for that of another they could hope to receive something of liberty by sovereign grace. The real liberty of Athens and her genuine democracy died with Demosthenes.

We know little of the more personal life of Demosthenes. He was married, and we know that he had one child, for Aeschines reproaches him for having appeared in public " with a garland on his head and white raiment on his body," rejoicing at the news of the death of Philip, when it was but seven days after the death of " the first and only one who ever called him ' father.' " As a boy he had been weak and awkward. His physique was not that of the typical Athenian, developed by gymnastic training. In his manhood he was abstemious, not a boon companion, always serious, indefatigable in the laborious preparation of his speeches. He did not like to speak offhand, and his published speeches testify to the infinite pains which he took in their revision. Probably as delivered on the bema they had more of the colloquial, perhaps too much of coarse and violent expression, for, statesman as he was, Demosthenes possessed all the arts of the demagogue; his years of experience in silencing and holding the restless, irresponsible crowd in the ecclesia had made him a master of popular oratory. There was in Demosthenes a vein of severity and fault-finding. Growing up under a standing grievance as a boy defrauded of his property, he seems to have acquired a censorious habit of mind. He is always stronger in attack than in defence — and he has no scruples which even suggest to him that one ought to ' fight fair.' Insinuation, perversion of the facts, outright falsehood if that will serve his purpose, are ready weapons with him — for he is an ugly fighter. Of course his enemies accused him of taking bribes — all Athenian politicians accused one another of that. His handling of the secret Persian subsidies and the scandal of the Harpalus affair gave color to the charge. But to us the abstemiousness of his life and the devotion with which he gave himself to the fight for his country's liberty, when the sure road to personal wealth and influence lay in the opposite direction, refute such accusations. He was a man of one supreme idea: that idea was the freedom of Athens and of Hellas. His disagreeable personal qualities are of little moment to those who appreciate the nobility of his political aims and the splendor of his oratory. He hated his political enemies, but he loved his country. He was capable of misrepresentation and abuse of his opponents, but he lifted the Athenian people to heights of idealism and patriotic sacrifice which recalled the days of Themistocles and Pericles, and made them worthy of their great ancestry.

II. THE ORATORY OF DEMOSTHENES

OUR manuscripts contain sixty speeches under the name of Demosthenes, but only about half of these are regarded by the critics as genuine. Thirteen of the genuine speeches are brief harangues delivered before the ecclesia. Some of the court speeches are essentially political in character, notably the long speeches *Against the Law of Leptines,* *On the Embassy,* and *On the Crown.* The speeches in private cases show some of the distinctive features of Demosthenes' oratory, but it is in the speeches on public affairs, whether delivered before the ecclesia or in the courts, that his full power is seen. It is unfortunate that so few of his many harangues before the ecclesia were published, and none of his addresses to assemblies in other states, to which he so often went to arouse Hellenic patriotism. The *Third Philippic* and the speech *On the Chersonese* are our greatest specimens of his popular harangues; the speech *On the Crown,* technically a court speech, has all the qualities both of a legal plea and a popular appeal, and it exhibits every phase of the Demosthenic oratory.

The plan of the political speeches depends in part, of course, upon the occasion of each. Brief harangues before the ecclesia, like the Olynthiacs and the Philippics, occupying from twenty to forty-five minutes in delivery, show a simple arrangement. In these brief speeches we find some one or two, occasionally three, main ideas, which are driven home again and again. Ideas like the aggressions of Philip and the supineness of the Athenians will be interwoven in repeated contrast and with sarcastic criticism — often with bitter attack on the speakers of the peace party. The plan is not to finish one topic and then present another, the more logical method, but to keep all before the hearers constantly, the more effective way to play upon the popular feeling.

The greater political speeches in court, some of them four hours long, required very different treatment, and here Demosthenes showed as complete mastery of strategy in arrangement as of skill in expression. He followed none of the set rules of the rhetoricians, by this time fully developed, but marshaled his material according to his own view of its effectiveness for attack and defence. His ' outline ' nowhere obtrudes — superficial readers say there is none — but a careful study shows that every part is placed according to a shrewd and deliberate plan.[3]

The speech *On the Crown* offered to Demosthenes the greatest difficulties, and it presents to us his supreme triumph. Demosthenes was the second speaker; all the long forenoon the jury had been listening to a review of his career, delivered by a man who had every reason for deadly hatred, and every facility for shrewd and persuasive attack. Demosthenes' whole career had been pictured as that of a man devoted only to his own advancement, whose leadership had led straight to Chaeronea and the loss of Greek liberty. Not content with branding him as a political failure and a shifty demagogue, Aeschines had declared him to be such an object of the divine displeasure that whatever his hand had touched — army, navy, cities — had become the victims of the wrath of heaven. The legal points which Aeschines had made were unanswerable; Demosthenes knew that both time and place of the proposed crowning were flatly against the law. His whole defence must rest upon a justification of his political career, a career which had culminated in Chaeronea, the death of a thousand Athenian citizens, and the loss of Athenian liberty. The only reasonable way to discuss his public life would be to treat it chronologically, but the first period had closed with Demosthenes' conspicuous activity in negotiating the detested Peace of Philocrates, and the last period had ended with the defeat at Chaeronea. How could a review of a statesman's services be successful if it must begin with one disaster, and end with another!

This was the situation which Demosthenes had to face as he sat down to draft the plan of his defence of Ctesiphon's motion and of his own leadership. His speech is one of the supreme triumphs of rhetorical strategy of arrangement and treatment. He decides upon the chronological order, but that unfortunate period of the making of the Philocratic Peace he labels as " outside the scope of the indictment." In fact it was not ' outside,' but by so representing it he throws the jury off their guard, and tempts them to give less critical attention to his account of the affair. Then,

denying that he himself was in any way responsible for the peace (the denial was an unblush-
ing falsehood, but the events were sixteen years
in the past, and few memories are as long as
that), and throwing the responsibility for all
the evil results of the peace upon Aeschines
himself, finally by a most brilliant muster-roll
of Greek traitors, followed by a witty personal
attack, he slips from under the odium of this
most unfortunate period, and shifts it onto the
head of his opponent, amid the applause of the
jury and the listeners outside the bar. Any
suspicion or hostile feeling that Aeschines' long
speech had left in the minds of the jury had
now been removed, or at any rate greatly miti-
gated. It was safe now to proceed straight to
the heart of the political question: Was Demosthenes' policy of opposition to Philip justified?

Demosthenes calls upon the clerk of the
court to read the indictment again. He then
draws a vivid picture of the states of Hellas at
the time when Philip's power was beginning to
threaten Greek freedom, and he challenges his
hearers with the question whether they would
have had Athens coöperate with Philip, or even
sit idly by while he was making himself lord

[52]

and master of all Greece. What was Old Athens to do when she saw the man from little Pella willing to sacrifice an eye, a hand, any part of his body that Fortune chose to call for, if only he might attain to glory and honor? As Philip was striding across all Hellas in violation of every pledge, was it not time for some one to hinder him? If some one, who but the people of Athens? There follows a rapid sketch of the successes of Demosthenes in checking Philip's progress: the rescue of Euboea, the Chersonese, and Byzantium. Deeds such as these were worthy of the sons of the men of old, whose pride it had always been to come to the rescue of any Hellenic state whose liberty was endangered — hostile though it might have been to Athens in the past — and to shrink from no peril when their own honor was at stake. The whole appeal lifts the thought of the hearers from questions of expediency and feasibility to the heights of national honor and pride, while by pausing in his chronological sketch just where he does, Demosthenes keeps the eyes of the jurors upon a period of real diplomatic and military success — Chaeronea is skilfully kept below the horizon. A brief sketch of Demosthenes' successful naval reforms confirms the good impression of the more eloquent appeal.

Now at last it is safe to take up the two legal technical questions, for which Demosthenes knows that he has no solid ground. Both of these he treats superficially and with an entire lack of candor. With a plausible answer to one and a contemptuous waiving aside of the other, he plunges into a personal attack upon Aeschines. The jury forget the weak legal defence in their delight in a delicious feast of personal abuse, and a malicious and slanderous caricature of the father and mother of Aeschines. The whole purpose is to hurry the jury away from any serious thought of the legal question, and to ride upon the tide of their laughter and applause at his vulgarities. Demosthenes knew his audience.

This piece of comedy prepares the way for a more serious attack upon Aeschines, beginning with a review of certain alleged disloyal acts, petty matters, but enough to lead up to the supreme attack: *Aeschines is himself responsible for Chaeronea and all the ruin which followed!* Thus Demosthenes completes his chronological review of events, but in such way that he is no longer defendant, but accuser.

The truth was that Chaeronea was the logical and inevitable result of Demosthenes' determined policy of coming to outright war with Philip. But by a supreme use of rhetorical art he makes it seem to the jury to be an interruption of the course of events, and to have been brought about by Aeschines' paid efforts in the service of Philip. The art of making 'the worse appear the better cause' was never used with more skill.[4]

But this is not all. Having shown that it was through acts of Aeschines that Philip was enabled to come unopposed through Thermopylae, Demosthenes proceeds in a most brilliant narrative to demonstrate that it was by his own negotiation with Thebes that Philip's march was arrested in Central Greece, and the final campaign kept off the soil of Attica itself. This splendid section, throwing the odium of the disaster upon Aeschines, and vindicating to Demosthenes the credit of bringing to his country at least a mitigation of the ruin which Aeschines had prepared for her, opens the way for the supreme challenge of the speech. " If the future had been foreseen by all, and all had foreknown, and you had forewarned us, Aeschines, and testified with shouts and cries —

you who did not open your mouth — not even so was our city to have drawn back from the contest, if she had any regard for glory, for her fathers, for future generations." The stupendous passage culminates in the famous Marathonian oath. With such consummate strategy Demosthenes turns what seemed inevitable personal defeat in argument, into triumph.

Demosthenes had now been speaking some two and one half hours. He had covered the whole ground with his arguments. It remained to reiterate the higher aspects of his policy, to review again and again his specific services, and to pour contempt upon his opponent from every possible standpoint. Here as always Demosthenes is depending upon moving the feelings of his hearers even more than convincing their reason. And so he adds one section after another, each a complete speech in itself, each reinforcing the effect of the main speech.

With a final contrast between his own conduct and that of Aeschines, the speaker closes with a prayer to the gods to grant rescue to the State from the overhanging fears.

The speech *On the Embassy,* an attack on Aeschines as guilty of treason, covered a smaller field of events, and offered a simpler problem of arrangement. Demosthenes here describes and attacks Aeschines' conduct in one situation after another, not altogether following chronological order, and, as he always likes to do, intermingling at each stage description, argument and invective.

In Demosthenes' civil cases before the courts there is the utmost variety in arrangement. Formal proem and epilogue we always find, but for the rest there is no set form.

In argumentation Demosthenes has all the proverbial Attic shrewdness and inventiveness. He has the ability to discover the central point of his case and to keep it steadily before the jury, by approaching it from every side and treating it in manifold ways. Not infrequently he is over-shrewd, drawing from an action or situation far-fetched conclusions, which are in danger of awakening the suspicion of the hearers rather than carrying conviction. He is not above misrepresenting the facts for the sake of the point he is determined to make. In case an argument of his is palpably weak, he is likely to rush into a furious personal attack, and to pour out a flood of sarcasm and ridicule on his opponent, trusting that in the storm of laughter which follows, the weakness of his logic will be carried away.

Demosthenes does not like long trains of argument; his experience on the bema had taught him that a popular audience will not follow them; and with the mob-jury of an Athenian court one had to confine himself to popular methods even in civil cases. His method is therefore to make a point by brief and rapid argument, and then to reinforce it by emotional appeal and often by sudden attack on his opponent. His longer speeches are therefore made up of a succession of short harangues, each with its narration, argument, emotional appeal, invective. Each section of this sort rises to a climax of argument, or oftener of feeling, and does its own work, while each wave of thought contributes its part to the steadily rising tide of emotion and conviction.

Commenting on the statement sometimes made that the speeches of Demosthenes are distinguished by great closeness of reasoning, Lord Brougham says: " If by this is only meant that he never wanders from the subject, that each remark tells upon the matter in hand, that all his illustrations are brought to bear upon the point, and that he is never found making any step in any direction which does not advance his main object and lead towards the conclusion to which he is striving to bring his hearers — the observation is perfectly just; for this is a distinguishing feature in the character of his eloquence. It is not, indeed, his grand excellence, because everything depends upon the manner in which he pursues this course, the course itself being one quite as open to the humblest mediocrity as to the highest genius. But if it is meant to be said that those Attic orators, and especially their great chief, made speeches in which long chains of elaborate reasoning are to be found — nothing can be less like the truth. A variety of topics are handled in succession, all calculated to strike the audience. Passions which predominated in their minds are appealed to — feelings easily excited among them are aroused by skilful allusions — glaring inconsistencies are shown in the advice given by others — sometimes by exhibiting the repugnance of those counsels among themselves, sometimes by contrasting them with other counsels proceeding from the same quarters. The pernicious tendency of certain measures is displayed by referring, sometimes, to the general principles of human action and the course

which human affairs usually take; more frequently, by a reference to the history of past,
and generally of very recent, events. Much invective is mixed with these topics, and both
the enemy without, and the evil counselor
within the walls, are very unsparingly dealt
with. . . . He was really speaking to them
respecting their own affairs, or rather respecting what they had just been doing or witnessing
themselves. Hence a very short allusion alone
was generally required to raise the idea which
he desired to present before his audience.
Sometimes a word was enough for his purpose;
the naming of a man or a town; the calling to
their recollection what had been done by the
one, or had happened to the other. . . . Such
apt allusion has a power — produces an elec-
trical effect — not to be reached by any chain
of reasoning, however close, and even the most
highly-wrought passages, and the most exquisite composition, fall far short of it in rous-
ing or controlling the minds of a large assembly. Chains of reasoning, examples of fine
argumentation, are calculated to produce their
effect upon a far nicer, a more confined, and a
more select audience."[5]

Demosthenes secures his greatest effects by

two most unlike appeals, the one the appeal to noble, generous civic pride and patriotism, the other, to the universal enjoyment which a mob finds in seeing a man pilloried with ridicule and invective. The appeals to patriotic pride are the crests of successive waves of eloquence in the speech *On the Crown.* " What was the adviser of the people to speak or to propose — I, the adviser at Athens, who knew that from the earliest times until the day on which I myself stepped upon the bema, my country had always struggled for leadership and honor and glory, and had spent more money and more lives for the sake of her own proud ambition and in the interest of all the Greeks than the other states had spent each for themselves! " (§ 66.) " If it was time for some one to stand forth to oppose these acts of Philip, who but the people of Athens was it to be? " (§ 72.) The Athenians of the old days " would not desert those who looked to them for safety, but they were willing to give themselves up to danger — a righteous and noble resolve. For death comes at last to every man, though he keep himself shut up in a closet. But the good man must lay his hand to every noble deed, trusting to the good shield of faith, and bear whatever heaven sends — nobly. This your fathers did." (§ 97.) " It cannot be, it cannot be, that you were mistaken, fellow-citizens, in choosing danger in behalf of the freedom and safety of all! No, in the name of those of our fathers who bore the brunt of the danger at Marathon, and those who stood in the ranks at Plataea, and those who fought in the ships at Salamis and at Artemisium, and many another who lies in the public tombs — GOOD MEN! " (§ 208.) " Each man of you, my fellow-citizens, ought to feel that when he takes up the juror's staff and ticket, he takes upon himself at the same moment the spirit of the city." (§ 210.) " If you talk of justified complaints of ours against the Thebans, or against the people of Byzantium or Euboea, or if you talk about equality now, first, you have never heard that when in olden times those ships fought for Hellas, three hundred in all, two hundred of them came from our city; and men saw her, not feeling that she was being over-reached, not putting on trial the men who advised her course, not angry at what was done, but grateful to heaven, if, when a common peril was impending upon the Greeks, she contributed twice as much as all the rest together for the common safety." (§ 238.)

The modern reader is astonished to find that
a man who had the statesmanlike insight and
the literary ability to lift the thoughts and feelings of his hearers to such heights could have
both will and ability to descend to the depths
of personal vituperation and abuse — and that
too in the same speech. The private civil cases
gave some opportunity for the exercise of this
ungodly talent, but it was in the public speeches
against his political enemies that Demosthenes
used every device of rhetoric to give pungency
and power to the outpourings of a rancorous
disposition. Indignation and suspicion, misrepresentation of every action, hatred and abuse,
find their full expression; and when both facts
and suspicion are too weak for his purpose, he
joyously turns to outright fabrication. The
classic instances of his lying abuse are the pic-
tures of Aeschines' boyhood and of the life of
his father and mother, as given in the speech
On the Crown. Thirteen years before, when
Aeschines' parents were still alive, Demosthenes had spoken of them with contempt —
the poor schoolmaster and the priestess of
silly rites. But now both are dead, and few of
the jury will remember them — and this time
Demosthenes is the last speaker; Aeschines

will have no opportunity to deny anything which he chooses to say. So now the father becomes the whipped slave of a schoolmaster, and the mother a noon-day prostitute! Less extended personal attacks are scattered all through the speech *On the Crown*. Sometimes they are genuine and fully justified bursts of indignation, at other times they are only to relieve the jury of the tedium of listening to long and serious argumentation, and always they are expressions of a deadly hatred of the man.

" Aeschines said somewhere in the course of his speech, as I remember, ' He who reproaches me with receiving the hospitality of Alexander.' I reproach you with the hospitality of Alexander? For what service, pray, or how did you deserve it? Neither Philip's guest nor Alexander's friend would I call YOU. I am not so crazy, unless, indeed, the harvest hands and the other hired men are to be called friends and guests of those who pay them their wages. No, far from it! But hireling of Philip of old, and today of Alexander I CALL YOU, and so do all these citizens. If you doubt it, ask them, or rather I will do it for you. Fellow-citizens, do you call Aeschines hireling, or guest, of Alexander? " The jury and the audience, carried

away by the wit of the rapid attack, shout
" Hireling! " Demosthenes turns to Aeschines,
who is sitting on the platform over against him,
" You hear what they say." (§ 51 ff.) " Do not
go around, my fellow-citizens, saying that Hellas has met such disasters at the hands of one
man. Not at the hands of one, but of many
men, and rascally men in every State, O Earth
and ye Gods! Of whom yonder man is one;
and if the truth ought to be spoken without
reserve, I should not hesitate to call him the
ruin of all that was lost thereafter, men, ter-
ritories, cities; for the man who furnishes the
seed, that man is responsible for the crop of
disasters." (§ 158 ff.)

Scattered all through the speech *On the
Crown* are opprobrious epithets, sudden flings,
bitter side remarks, often the more effective because inserted in some piece of elevated appeal
or solid argumentation. " Puppy . . . slanderer, scandal-monger, arrant tragic ape, rascal,
enemy of the gods, . . . bawling and shouting
. . . pompous orator . . . pest . . . you ac-
cursed round-shouldered clerk . . . you miserable actor . . . traitor . . . stupid . . . despicable. . . . What could a man call you! "

Ivo Bruns, in his brilliant book *Das litera-*

rische Porträt der Griechen, has traced the development of literary portraiture from Thucydides down through Aristophanes, Plato, Lysias, and the rest, to the time of Demosthenes. He shows that this art in the works of the Greek orators and politicians degenerates into studied caricature and abuse, and that it reaches its depth of misrepresentation in Demosthenes. Of Demosthenes' characterization of Midias and Aeschines he says (p. 585): " Between the actuality of these men and our eyes, falsehood lies like an impenetrable veil;" of the characterization of Aeschines (p. 571): " The picture is everywhere the same: a war to the death, with poisoned weapons."

This field of abuse and sarcasm, in which Demosthenes is certainly a master, seems to have exhausted his capacity for wit. He is too stern and too intense for humor, and the pleasant play of wit does not appeal to him. With Demosthenes wit is a weapon, not an ornament or a relaxation.

A third characteristic of Demosthenes' oratory is his insight in the analysis of a political situation, and his presentation of it in speech so simple and clear that the common man must see the point at issue, and feel the urgency of the case. This involved on the part of the orator the penetration of a statesmanlike mind, and consummate art of composition. In the early days of Philip's progress, when other public men in Athens were only mildly curious about the rumors of the doings of another Macedonian princeling in the remote north, Demosthenes was already discerning the marvelous ability of the man and his outreaching ambition. In later years Demosthenes made faithful study of the situation of the other States, each in some peculiar relation to Philip, and he was constantly expounding to his fellow-citizens these ever changing situations. Much of his power of leadership lay in this superior discernment and masterly analysis in popular address. This, already evident in the earliest *Philippics*, reaches its height in the *Crown Speech*, where again and again he justifies his own acts by analysis of one situation after another. Why was the Peace of Philocrates made? He passes in rapid review all the circumstances: the Phocian War, Athenian hatred of Thebes, the factions in the Peloponnesus, the lavish bribes of Philip — buying traitors in every state, his plausible offers, the supine indifference of the Greek States in general. In thirty lines of our text we read the whole story (§§ 18 ff.). This was the real introduction to the great speech, and served as foundation for all that followed. Later in the same argument in an equally striking analysis he sums up the influences which thwarted all his own efforts: " But the cities were sick, the men in public life and responsibility bribed and corrupted for money; the private citizens and the masses partly not foreseeing, partly baited by the ease and leisure of the day, and all in some such condition as this: each thinking that the danger was coming, but not upon themselves, and that through other men's perils their own safety would be secured whenever they pleased. Accordingly, I think, the outcome has been that the masses, as the price of their great and untimely ease, have lost their freedom; and the leaders, who thought they were selling out everything but themselves, have discovered that their own persons were the first thing that they had sold. For instead of being called friends and guests, the names they were called when they were taking bribes, now they are termed flatterers, enemies of the gods, and all the other names that fit them." (§§ 45 ff.) When, in the great central section of his argument, he flings out

the challenge "Was not some one to stand
forth for the freedom of Hellas? If some one,
who but the people of Athens?", he traverses
the whole field again: the 'crop of traitors' in
every state, Philip's policy of bribing and di-
viding, the obligation of Athenians to cherish
the traditions of the fathers, the communities
which, seeking only their immediate and selfish
ends, have been ruined thereby, the glorious
deeds of Old Athens in behalf of other states,
Philip's own willingness to sacrifice everything
else to the attainment of glory, the reminders
of the great days of the fathers 'in every
speech and spectacle,' the swift aggressions of
Philip and the long list of his encroachments.

Such analyses carry their own argumentative
force; they are themselves arguments, and they
contribute much to that impression of mastery,
of wide vision, which we receive in reading the
speeches.

An important factor in such analysis of
political situations was Demosthenes' command
of the facts of history. Not only was he steeped
in the narrative and the interpretative speeches
of the *History* of Thucydides, and in the story
of those earlier events which were on the
tongue of every orator, Marathon, Salamis,

Plataea, but he had followed all the later efforts of his country, her swift recovery after the Peloponnesian War, her resistance to Thebes, her repeated efforts to hold control of Euboea, — that long 'rampart' over against the Attic coast — her late relations with Persia. Just as in his pleas in the civil courts Demosthenes shows himself a master of legal precedent, so in the political speeches he is constantly appealing to the example of the fathers, calling upon his hearers to play their part manfully in the age-long, consistent struggle of Athens for glory and honor.

In the use of general maxims, those sententious precepts in which are condensed long human experience and the common consent of mankind, Demosthenes is not lavish, but when the case demands such support, it is given with all the more force. As to his method of introducing them, Butcher's discerning statement is admirable: " Among the causes which give to the eloquence of Demosthenes and Burke an enduring value beyond any other eloquence, ancient or modern, none is to be ranked above this, that a close grappling with detail is found combined with large generalizations from experience and the broad assertion of moral truths."

. . . But their method is not the same; "Burke often expounds [general principles] in the manner of a philosopher — the secret of many of his failures in Parliament. In Demosthenes the principle gradually emerges from the facts. It is not supplied as a thing ready made. . . . As the facts are presented first on one side then on another, the illuminating principle breaks in." (Butcher, *Demosthenes*, p. 154.) In the earlier Philippic speeches such general principles and maxims are rather frequent, and sometimes they are elaborated with considerable detail. (cf. *Olynth.*, II. 9 ff., 21) The *Leptinea*, a speech dealing with the necessity of preserving national good-faith and of giving suitable rewards to benefactors, naturally calls out numerous general statements of right and policy. On the other hand the speech *On the Embassy*, a rapid and virulent personal attack, has no place for them. The speech *On the Crown*, while very sparing in the use of such expressions, has some splendid instances in its higher ranges: "A man in his private capacity, and a state in its wider sphere, must always try to make present conduct conform to the best precedents of the past." (§ 95.) "Death awaits us all, even though a man keep himself shut up in a closet. But the good man must lay his hand to every honorable deed, trusting to the good shield of faith, and he must bear whatever God sends, NOBLY." (§ 97.) " He who believes that he was born to his parents only, awaits that death which comes in the inevitable order of nature; but he who believes that he was born for his country as well, will be willing to die that he may not see her enslaved, and the insults and dishonor which one must bear in a city en- slaved, he will hold more terrible than death." (§ 205.) "The man who serves those from whom his country apprehends some peril to herself, lies not at the same anchorage with the people, nor looks for safety from the same source." (§ 281.)

Athenian legal practitioners were constantly called upon to write speeches for clients to de- liver in the courts under the fiction that they had been written with their own pen, instead of bought and paid for. To make such a speech conform to the personal characteristics of the man who was to deliver it, was one of the essen- tials of the lawyer's art. In this ' ethopoiia ' the art of narrative played a large part, and Lysias' unapproached supremacy in this field was due

in no small degree to his ability in narration.
Here Demosthenes is not at home. In any one
of the numerous speeches written for clients
to deliver, it is the same man who is speaking,
Demosthenes himself; he cannot submerge
himself in the personality of his client; it is
Demosthenes' own point of view that is presented in the speech, his own argumentative
style which stands out. It was only in the more
serious private cases, having also something of
political significance, that Demosthenes' sober
and often indignant style so far fitted the character of the speaker and the circumstances of
the case as to carry conviction.

The speeches of Demosthenes do not abound
in extensive narrative or description. The orator is too intent upon pressing his point, too
fond of argumentation, too rapid in his movement to give much place to picturesque narrative, or any place at all to merely epideictic
description. Where he narrates, as he often
does, each step of the narrative is usually
coupled with comment or argument, and we
are not allowed to lose sight of the speaker himself. With Lysias it is very different. He tells
the story of a series of acts in a way so simple,
vivid, and apparently objective that argument

seems superfluous; we see the act through the eyes of the speaker, and our minds have reached his conclusion before he announces it. Aeschines, too, trained on the stage, has a liking for picturesque and moving narrative, and is second to Lysias only in ability to compose it. Demosthenes can seldom vie with either of these men. And yet his clearness, simplicity, and rapidity do enable him at times to approach perfection even here. His highest point is reached in the famous description of the consternation at Athens on receipt of the news that Philip had fortified Elatea. (*De Cor.*, §§ 169 ff.) In a narrative of fourteen lines the reader finds himself in the midst of events, excited, anxious, eager for the outcome. Then the narrative begins to be interspersed with comment, description with interpretation. In the strictly narrative part of this great passage the purity and simplicity are equal to the best Lysian standard; the quick transition to comment and argument is characteristically Demosthenic.

A reading of all the extant speeches of Demosthenes will show that we have in them no extended narrative or description that can be compared with the story of the old man Diogiton in Lysias, the scene at Delphi in Aeschines, the raid of Hadir Ali on the Carnatic as described by Burke, or Webster's description of the murder of Captain Joseph White.

In appeal to the feelings, Demosthenes' power in stirring the great emotions of patriotism and love of personal honor, as well as the severe emotions of indignation and anger, has been sketched already. In the appeal to the weaker emotions, pity, sympathy, fear, he is always restrained, perhaps by his artistic standards, quite as likely by peculiarities of his own temperament. Here he is in marked contrast with the ex-actor Aeschines. There is nothing in the speeches of Demosthenes that can be compared with Aeschines' lament over the strange, supernatural misfortunes which in these late years have befallen Hellas and the world, or his threnody over ruined Thebes.[6]

The force and dignity of Demosthenes' oratory are very largely the result of his command of the periodic style. The oratorical 'period' gathers together the subordinate elements of a complex idea, or its several parallel elements, compacting and rounding out the whole in such way that the hearer feels from the first that all these elements are contributing to one commanding thought. At each stage of the sentence he feels that more is to follow, and that what he has already heard is to find its full meaning in what is to come. Compactness and the rounding out of some conception, the holding of the attention to each individual element as a part of a complete idea, are of the essence of periodic structure.

The rhetoricians of the fifth century had already begun the study of the periodic style. Gorgias had developed and played with the sharp, striking type which consists in antithesis. Thrasymachus had taught the theory of a larger periodic style, and Lysias had developed it to a considerable extent in practice. Then in Demosthenes' own time Isocrates had brought to perfection that type of period which rests upon amplification of thought, expressed with symmetrical parallelism of form. These stately and perfectly shaped periods of Isocrates, as symmetrical as a Doric portico, reach the height of epideictic beauty, but nothing could be less adapted to the court room and the ecclesia. It remained for Demosthenes to shape a periodic style that should have amplitude of thought combined with compact and rounded structure, and with intensity and striking force. Demosthenes is equally at home in shaping the short, sharp antithetic period, the larger symmetrical group of parallel clauses, or that strongest form in which by the presentation first of the subordinate thoughts, perhaps in a dozen clauses, the hearer's mind is held in intense expectation of that clause which is to give force and meaning to the whole.[7] It is in the shaping of such periods of *sensus suspensio* that Demosthenes is the master of ancient and modern orators. He knows none of the rules restricting length which the later rhetoricians laid down. He amplifies the preliminary and subordinate thoughts until our mind is intent with expectation and our emotions deeply stirred, then comes the strong impact of that idea which all that has preceded is to drive home to mind and heart.[8]

As Demosthenes shows the utmost variety in form and length of periods, he is also farthest removed from monotony in the use of the periodic type. He seldom has a succession of long periods; the large period stands out by its very isolation. The periodic effect of a page of one of Demosthenes' speeches is due not so much to a succession of periodic sentences as to the constant play of antithesis, the placing of the subordinate clause before the principal one (the simplest form of *sensus suspensio*), and the parallelism of several coördinate clauses, all within sentences which as a whole are of the non-periodic type.

The longer periods are noteworthy for the skill with which they are compacted. An inflected language gives greater facility in such structure; the members of a phrase can be so separated as to hold together a large complex of thought, and the emphatic word of the whole can be placed wherever the speaker chooses. Much of this is lost in translation; no reader of Demosthenes in English can hope to feel anything like the real force of his periods.

Where the volume of a period is too great for the hearer to keep all in mind until the culminating kola give the clue to the whole, Demosthenes knows how to excite a feeling, an emotion, which does carry on, even while we forget the individual statements; we need only give ourselves up to the rising feeling. Indeed, it is to moving the feelings rather than convincing the reason that the periodic style is adapted. Demosthenes has a fine instinct in this, and he controls the simplest non-periodic style where the appeal is entirely to the understanding.

Amplification, the expansion of a thought for rhetorical effect, is one of the most common means for giving strength and dignity to periodic structure, as well as for reinforcing a single word or phrase. The restraint of Demosthenes, as compared with Cicero and the classical English orators, is here especially marked.[9] Certain of his great periods, like the one cited in note 8, are built on extended amplification, and are models of its use, but there is no indulgence in the showy form of expression merely for display. If Demosthenes pours out a long stream of details, it is to arouse the feeling of the hearer steadily and irresistibly, till he is carried away by the concluding thought. These great periods are the more effective for being rarely used. In non-periodic sentences amplification often plays a large part in presenting a fact in all its aspects, or merely in holding the attention to a simple idea by expressing it in repeated synonyms.

A common and effective form of amplification is the strengthening of an idea by coupling with it its negatived opposite. " Philip hires this despicable man, no longer in common with

the other ambassadors, but all by himself."
(*De Cor.*, § 33.) " Among the Greeks, not some,
but all alike." (*De Cor.*, § 61.) "Compare your
life and mine, gently, not bitterly, Aeschines."
(*De Cor.*, § 265.) The simplest form of amplification, the use of two synonymous words
where one would suffice to express the essential
idea, is so common in Demosthenes as to become a mannerism; sometimes it is quite impossible to justify his pairs of words. We find
them everywhere, often with a significant difference in the force of the two words, but sometimes with no difference whatever: " Now this
you must see and examine." (*Embassy*, § 30.)
" I will tell you this and shew you." (*Phil.*, I.
§ 22.) "We are forced to acknowledge and
admit." (*De Chers.*, § 35.)

Antithesis, whether it be the contrast of ideas
naturally opposed, or the purely rhetorical setting of one form of expression over against another, is one of the strongest and finest instruments of intense oratory. It appealed especially
to the Greeks, and from the time of Antiphon
on, their oratory is full of it. A plaything in
the hands of Gorgias, it became a plastic element of Isocrates' symmetrical periods. Demosthenes uses it in every possible form, and for

every purpose, — exposition, noble appeal, reproach, denunciation, mockery, ridicule: now
in a long series of contrasted kola, now in a
sharp, brief pair, again in a single word set over
against another. The intensity with which he
usually speaks and the tone of censure which
is so prevalent with him find expression in this
rhetorical ' figure ' above all others:

" *Compare side by side your life and mine, gently,
    not bitterly, Aeschines: . . .*
You *were a schoolmaster,*
I *was a scholar;*
You *served in the initiations,*
I *was an initiate;*
You *were a clerk,*
I *was a voter;*
You *were a third-rate actor,*
I *was a spectator;*
You *broke down,*
I *hissed.*
All *your political acts have been for our enemies,*
Mine, *for my country." (De Cor., § 265.)* [10]

The sharp, nervous rhetorical question is
particularly adapted to Demosthenes' vigorous
style. The sleepy hearer is aroused, the indifferent is challenged, even the stupid man is
tempted to try to think, when the sudden ques-

tion is thrown in his face. Often question and answer fly back and forth between Demosthenes and a supposed objector. Often the question is so framed that any answer save the one that Demosthenes intends, would be absurd. The language is often colloquial and oaths abound:

When, fellow-citizens, when will you do your duty? "When, by Zeus, necessity arises." But what ought we to call that which is going on today? I think to the free man the greatest ' necessity ' is shame at a situation in which he finds himself. Tell me, do you wish to stroll around inquiring of one another, " Is there any news? " What greater ' news ' could there be than that a man of Macedon is defeating Athenian troops, and administering the affairs of Hellas? " Is Philip dead? " " No, by Zeus, but he's sick." What difference does that make to you? If anything happens to him, you'll speedily create another Philip, if this is the way you are going to attend to your business. For it is not his own energy that has exalted him, so much as your neglect. (*Phil.*, I. §§ 10 ff. Cf. *De Chers.*, § 17.)

The vigor of Demosthenes' rapid thought finds frequent expression in metaphorical language, most often in a single word or a brief phrase. The fully expanded simile is rare, but shaped with wonderful skill. The intermediate form, the word or phrase introduced by "like" (ὥσπερ), is used sparingly, but with exquisite appropriateness and striking force.

The interests of Athens "have been toasted away in return for the pleasure and gratification of the moment." (*Olynth.*, III. § 22.) Philip is "drunk" with the magnitude of his successes. (*Phil.*, I. § 49.) "The cities were sick, . . . the masses baited by the ease and leisure of the moment." (*De Cor.*, § 45.) The politicians "have cut the sinews of the people, and they tame them and break them to harness." (*Olynth.*, III. § 31.) Philip is steadily "encircling us and casting his net about us." (*Phil.*, I. § 9.) "In all the advice I have given my fellow citizens never have I advised them, as you have done, tipping like a scale-beam to the weight of gain." (*De Cor.*, § 298.) "It is not possible, it is not possible, fellow-citizens, by a course of wrong-doing and perjury and lying to acquire lasting power; such prosperity prevails for the moment, for a little while, and blossoms with hope, it may be, but time searches it out and the flower of it withers away." (*Olynth.*, II. § 10.) The imminent danger from Philip would

have fallen on Athens "like a cloud-burst."
(*De Cor.*, § 153.) Demosthenes' decree "caused
the danger that was impending over Athens
to pass away — like a cloud (ὥσπερ νέφος)."
(*De Cor.*, § 188.) In characterizing the traitors
in the Greek states Demosthenes throws off his
usual restraint, and one metaphor follows another in rapid succession: " Men polluted, flatterers, destructive, who have mutilated each his
fatherland, who have toasted away their freedom formerly to Philip, and now to Alexander,
who measure their prosperity by their belly and
their shame, while freedom and independence
of any lord and master, which to the Greeks of
olden time were the metes and bounds of happi-
ness, they have overthrown." (*De Cor.*, § 296.)
Aeschines, silent when we needed advice, vocif-
erous in criticism when disaster has befallen,
is like a physician who has no word of advice
for his sick patient, but who, when the poor
fellow has perished, follows to the grave and
demonstrates how if the man had done this
thing and that, he would not have died. (*De
Cor.*, § 243.) . . . The Athenians fight Philip
precisely as a barbarian boxes: hit the barbarian, and his hand comes up only in time to
rub the spot that was hit; hit him in another

place, there come his hands! But to ward off a blow or to see it coming, he has neither knowledge nor concern. (*Phil.*, I. § 40.)

In addition to these natural and dignified instruments of eloquence, the rhetoricians of the Gorgian school had a bag full of the tricks of sound and jingle: pairs of rhyming kola, play on the sound of words with every possible punning device, successive kola beginning or ending with the same word, a kolon having the same word for its beginning and its close (called the ' circle,' κύκλος). The reader of Greek finds all these in our fragments of the work of Gorgias, some of them in the speeches of Isocrates. The reader of English has only to turn to John Lyly and his *Euphues* to find them all brought over into the English of the Elizabethan period.[11] Now any man who had been trained in the current rhetoric as Demosthenes certainly had been, knew and used the Gorgian tricks of the trade; but it is characteristic of Demosthenes' feeling for the adaptation of sound and form to sense, and his experience in the practical oratory of the courts and the ecclesia, that he uses these things very sparingly, and each of them for something better than display. Rhyming kola he does not like.

While to the Greek, a stranger to rhyme as a regular ornament of poetry, rhyme in prose had no such suggestion of verse as it has to us, it did give a touch of artificiality, while Demosthenes loves directness and force. Demosthenes is not without his *paronomasia*, the punning play on sound, but he reserves this for sarcastic attack or ridicule, where he seeks to raise a laugh. Other speakers used it as an ornament of their most serious thought. The ' ladder ' ($\kappa\lambda\hat{\iota}\mu\alpha\xi$) of the rhetoricians has but one instance in Demosthenes, but that is an effective and famous one:

" I *did not speak thus, and fail to make the motion,*
I *did not make the motion, and fail to go on the embassy,*
I *did not go on the embassy, and fail to persuade the Thebans."* (*De Cor.*, § 179.)

Anaphora, the use of the same word at the beginning of successive kola, is rare in the elegant periods of Isocrates, but Demosthenes uses it often, and with tremendous effect:

" *It was not safe in Olynthus to speak in behalf of Philip*
until the fruits of his capture of Potidaea had been bestowed on the Olynthian people;

It was not safe in Thessaly to speak in behalf of Philip
until the masses of the Thessalians had been helped by Philip's expulsion of their tyrants, and his restoration of the Pylaea to them;
It was not safe in Thebes,
until he had restored to them Boeotia and uprooted the Phocians;
But at Athens, when Philip has not only robbed us of Amphipolis and the Cardian land, but is preparing Euboea as a rampart against you, and is now moving on Byzantium,
IT IS SAFE TO SPEAK IN BEHALF OF PHILIP."
(*De Chers.,* §§ 64 ff.)

"*Up to that point Lasthenes was named*
'*friend,*'
until he betrayed Olynthus;
up to that point Timolas,
until he ruined Thebes;
up to that point Eudikus and Simus of Larisa,
until they brought Thessaly under Philip;
then, driven out and insulted, and suffering what not misery, they have been scattered to the ends of the earth." (*De Cor.,* § 48.)

[87]

The principle of the avoidance of hiatus, that "gaping" of the lips which comes when a vowel at the end of a word is followed by a vowel at the beginning of the next word, had become recognized in Greek poetry, and was becoming established in the more elegant prose style in the first half of the fourth century. Isocrates carried the rule so far that he would not allow hiatus even when two words were separated by a full pause. The objectionable concurrence of vowels was avoided by elision, crasis, and the skilful placing of words. Only with certain small words, and that within a narrow range, is hiatus found in Isocrates' fully polished works. Demosthenes, combining here as everywhere the precepts of the schools with the results of practical experience of his own, followed in general the law of avoidance of hiatus, but he saw that at a pause between kola, or at the end of a sentence, hiatus was in no way objectionable to the ear, and here he permitted it freely, as well as with many of the small particles and the article " the."

A still more subtle refinement of composition, not noticed by the ancient critics, but discovered in our own time by Friedrich Blass, is Demosthenes' avoidance of a succession of three or more short syllables. Apparently he felt that such movement was not fitted to the strong march of his appeals. Not infrequently he goes to the extreme of an almost unbroken succession of long syllables throughout a kolon. Of course the avoidance of the groups of short syllables has its exceptions: a group within a word cannot be avoided, and if the word is needed, Demosthenes does not hesitate to use it; before a pause the last syllable of a group is so naturally lengthened that there can be no objection to such a series; certain necessary groups of words, such as article and noun, or preposition and its object, were allowed even though they gave three or more short syllables. But, allowing for all such classes of exceptions, and for apparent groups which are removed by elision, crasis, or other turn of pronunciation, we find that in Demosthenes' most carefully prepared speeches other groups of short syllables are very rare indeed. In the speech *On the Crown* we find on the average only 6 groups to the (Teubner) page; the speech *On the Chersonese* shows 4.3 to the page; the *Third Philippic*, 9.4. How surely this is the result of a definite attempt to avoid such groups is seen by comparison with the work of authors who evidently wrote without regard to such effect. An average page of Thucydides shows 50 such groups, of Lysias 47, of Isocrates 39, of Aeschines 40. Comparing these with the 6 of the *De Corona* we see that we are dealing with a very definite principle of composition. How far this finally may have become unconscious with Demosthenes we cannot say; doubtless it was increasingly so.

To a modern student it is astonishing to find a man who is so intent on the cause he is pleading, and who passes so rapidly from one style of speech to another, applying to his language such refinements of style as the avoidance of hiatus and of a succession of short syllables. Here we see at its best the fine Attic taste and exquisite sense of the relation of sound to thought.[12]

Undoubtedly there is also in the speeches of Demosthenes a very definite effect of rhythm, varying with the changing movement of the thought. The importance of rhythm in prose, clearly distinct from the rhythms of poetry, was already recognized by the rhetoricians. Syllabic quantity, stress, and pitch all must have contributed to this prose rhythm. The ancient critics, Dionysius of Halicarnassus especially, expatiate on the rhythmical movement of Demosthenes' periods. But thus far modern scholars have made little progress toward discovering the secret of it. It is one of the open questions for students of Greek oratory; volumes have been written on it in recent years, but no agreement has been reached.[13]

In Demosthenes' opinion, if we may trust an anecdote told in Cicero's *Brutus* (142), the supreme requirement for effective oratory was DELIVERY. " What, Demosthenes, is first in oratory? " " Delivery." " What is second? " " Delivery." " What third? " " Delivery." We have abundant testimony to the fact that Demosthenes' delivery was as powerful as his thought. Not only had he attained mastery of voice, but his whole body reinforced his words. Aeschines ridicules his excited gestures, the violent movements of his whole body — " spinning around on the bema " — his shouts, his tears. The modern scholar, reading Demosthenes in his study, must in imagination transport himself to the Athenian court-room, where five hundred, a thousand, fifteen hundred men of the ordinary citizenship are sitting as jurors, while outside the bar the great spaces of the hall are filled with a throng of listeners, not Englishmen or Americans, but excitable, keen-witted, passionate Athenians; or he must imagine himself in the crowded ecclesia on the hill Pnyx, where the destiny of the State itself may be hanging this morning on the words of that tall, spare, severe man, who sways the people as the wind sways the ripe grain on the hillsides. Words and gestures are addressed not to the scholar and the critic in his study, but to the great mass of common men. And yet, never have words been written — refined even to the euphony of vowels and the balancing of the quantity of a syllable — that have more triumphantly stood the test of the world's critical scholarship.

All the rhetorical devices and all the powers of argumentation which have been enumerated are so used as to give the impression of variety and rapidity. It is true that certain characteristics stand out as predominant: earnestness, severity, elevation; but with these, relieving the emotion, holding the attention, delighting the imagination, is the play of a most versatile mind. The later critics fixed upon the word δεινότης, *power,* as descriptive of Demosthenes' oratory. From the time of the Sophists the

[92]

term δεινὸς λέγειν had been the title of the trained speaker and debater. The term δεινότης as applied to Demosthenes' oratory means that he is the Master of the Art, and that power is the essence of it. Dionysius gives to him the name " Proteus." When Menelaus was thwarted in his attempt to pursue his homeward voyage from Egypt, he had to seize and hold the Old Man of the Sea, Proteus of Egypt, who struggled desperately to escape his captors, turning now into a bearded lion, then into a dragon, then into a leopard, a big boar, a stream of water, a branching tree. The Demosthenic ability lies largely in the " power " to make the protean changes from one type of speech and appeal to another with a rapidity which defies capture, giving to the hearers no time for counter reflection, no .occasion for weariness, but sweeping the whole audience along at the will of the speaker.

Lord Brougham, speaking in his *Eloquence of the Ancients* (p. 41) of the " exquisite taste " of the Athenian audience, says: " It may be remarked generally, that a speaker who thinks to lower his composition in order to accommodate himself to the habits and taste of his audience, when addressing the multitude,

[93]

will find that he commits a grievous mistake. All the highest powers of eloquence consist in producing passages which may at once affect even the most promiscuous assembly; but even the graces of composition are not thrown away upon such auditors. Clear, strong, terse, yet natural and not strained expressions; happy antitheses; apt comparisons; forms of speech which are natural without being obvious; harmonious periods, yet various, spirited, and never monotonous or too regularly balanced: — these are what will be always sure to captivate every audience, and yet in these mainly consists finished, and elaborate, and felicitous diction." In the closing words of the same essay the English orator gives a splendid characterization of the oratory of the greatest of the Greeks: "At the head of all the mighty masters of speech, the adoration of ages has consecrated his place; and the loss of the noble instrument with which he forged and launched his thunders, is sure to maintain it unapproachable forever. If in such varied and perfect excellences it is required that the most prominent shall be selected, then doubtless is the palm due to that entire and uninterrupted devotion which throws his whole soul into his subject, and will

not ever — no, not for an instant — suffer a
rival idea to cross its resistless course without
being swiftly swept away and driven out of
sight. . . . So, too, there is no coming back
on the same ground, any more than any lin-
gering over it. Why should he come back over
a territory that he has already laid waste —
where the consuming fire has left not a blade
of grass? All is done at once; but the blow is
as effectual as it is single, and leaves not anything to do. There is nothing superfluous —
nothing for mere speaking's sake — no topic
that can be spared by the exigency of the business in hand; so, too, there seems none that can
be added — for everything is there and in its
place. So, in the diction, there is not a word
that could be added without weakening, or
taken away without marring, or altered without
changing its nature, and impairing the character of the whole exquisite texture, the work of a
consummate art that never for a moment ap-
pears, nor ever suffers the mind to wander from
the subject, and fix itself on the speaker. All is
at each instant moving forward, regardless of
every obstacle. The mighty flood of speech rolls
on in a channel ever full, but which never over-
flows. Whether it rushes in a torrent of allu-

sions, or moves along in a majestic exposition of enlarged principles — descends hoarse and headlong in overwhelming invective — or glides melodious in narrative and description, or spreads itself out shining in illustration — its course is ever onward and ever entire; — never scattered — never stagnant — never sluggish. At each point manifest progress has been made, and with all that art can do to charm, to strike, and to please. No sacrifice, even the smallest, is ever made to effect — nor can the hearer ever stop for an instant to contemplate or to admire, or throw away a thought upon the great artist, till all is over, and the pause gives time to recover his breath. This is the effect, and the proper effect of Eloquence — it is not the effect of argument. The two may be well combined, but they differ specifically from each other."

III. THE INFLUENCE OF DEMOS-
THENES IN CLASSICAL
ANTIQUITY

BY the time of Demosthenes it had become customary for orators to publish their speeches, sometimes in order to influence public opinion by reaching a wider circle than that of the hearers, often simply as specimens of oratory and for use in the studies of the schools of rhetoric. Without doubt Demosthenes revised and published some of his political speeches as soon as they were delivered; others were probably published during his lifetime; still others, which evidently lack final revision, in some cases being manifestly only first drafts, were doubtless found among his effects and published by his literary executors. Finally these scattered and partial collections were gathered into a comprehensive edition, which included also a considerable number of speeches which had come to be ascribed to him, but are clearly by other authors. It is uncertain just where and when this comprehensive collection was made and published, whether at Athens or Alexandria,[14] but the Alexandrian library certainly had such an edition within a century after the orator's death. The collection once made, copies of it were widely distributed. The speeches of Demosthenes, whether in editions of a few related speeches, or in complete collections, were therefore to be found everywhere in the libraries, and often in private possession. They were widely read, and were used in the instruction of the schools of rhetoric throughout the Greek and Roman world.

In spite of the decline of real oratory after the fall of Greek liberty, the schools of rhetoric flourished. Already in the lifetime of Demosthenes the fragmentary precepts of the new art of rhetoric had been brought together, systematized, and given a sound philosophic basis by Aristotle, whose *Rhetoric* became the starting-point for the many and more elaborate treatises of the succeeding generations. In Aristotle's *Rhetoric* the oratory of Demosthenes plays no part — he is never quoted — whether because Aristotle, the intimate friend of Philip and tutor of Alexander, looked upon Demosthenes as a mischievous demagogue and his oratory as the perversion of public speech to

[98]

evil uses, or because the examples of eloquence which Aristotle used in the *Rhetoric* were taken from rhetorical collections made before Demosthenes had become famous. Certainly the *Rhetoric* of Aristotle did nothing to perpetuate the influence of Demosthenes' oratory.

The surviving fragments of the rhetorical treatises which were written in the first centuries after Aristotle are so small that we are unable to determine how far their authors used Demosthenes' speeches as examples of eloquence, or quoted from them in defining and illustrating the 'figures' of rhetoric. We do know that the tendency of these rhetorical schools was now toward the florid, exhibition (epideictic) type of oratory. We can safely assume that the showy style of Gorgias and Isocrates was more to their taste than the sinewy, nervous, stern type of Demosthenes; and the young men who were frequenting the rhetorical schools of decadent Athens, or the Asianized schools of Rhodes, Pergamum, and Alexandria, were not seeking facility in swaying free political assemblies — there were no free assemblies any more — or in moving a jury of their peers — the courts of that day were moved, not by eloquence, but by influence and gold. The young students of oratory were seeking ability to win applause by eloquent declamation or flattering eulogy. The study of Demosthenes would contribute little to their training. Yet for sixty years after the death of Demosthenes there was a considerable body of citizens who cherished the ideals of national independence and leadership to which Demosthenes had devoted his life. More than once they persuaded the people to take up arms in the attempt to throw off the overlord, or at least to maintain a semblance of autonomy. Fruitless as all these efforts proved, they did serve to perpetuate the memory and the words of the great patriot. In the first century after his death one of the most influential of the patriot leaders was his sister's son, Demochares, politician, orator, and historian. In 280–79 B.C. he carried a decree by which a bronze statue of Demosthenes was to be set up in the agora, and the oldest member of each generation of his descendants was to enjoy the honor of a seat at the public table in the Prytaneum. The speeches of a nephew thus devoted to the memory of Demosthenes must have done something to keep his words alive for at least one generation. There is mention also of a Thessalian, Kineas, who had heard Demosthenes, and who so powerfully imitated his vigor and strength that he more than any other man of his time reminded the people of Demosthenes himself.

It is impossible to say how far the memory and influence of Demosthenes persisted in the popular mind through the third century, a time of political confusion for Athens, when hopeless attempts to secure something of self government ended in utter prostration. The general tendency of the century was away from his ideals. Quiet and safety could best be secured by submitting to an outside power. On the bema a new type of oratory held sway. Within four years of the death of Demosthenes both public policies and public speech had come under the powerful influence of an Athenian whose aim was to administer the city as a loyal servant of Macedon, and who was the founder of a new type of public speech. This man, Demetrius of Phalerum, from 318 to 307 B.C. governor of Athens under Macedon, supported by the anti-democratic element in his own city, was the most effective public speaker of his time. In a published treatise on rhetoric and in frequent speeches he sought an oratorical style midway between the simplicity of Lysias, and the vehement, nervous, rapid style of Demosthenes. He criticised the long, symmetrical periods of Isocrates, and made his own periods shorter and simpler, yet not approaching the Lysian simplicity.

It is probable then that throughout the third century three types of practical oratory were heard on the Athenian bema: the Demosthenic, nervous, rapid, passionate, powerful, but from the first sadly weakened by the inferior natural ability of Demosthenes' patriot successors, and less and less often heard as the patriot cause was seen to be almost hopeless; then there was the Isocratic type, admirably adapted to orations of flattery and encomium, for which there was only too frequent occasion; and there was the third type, the Demetrian, clear, forceful, elegant, adapted to the ordinary occasions of political life — a very practical type of public speech.

During the second century B.C. there was nothing in the public life of Athens that could tend to revive Demosthenic ideals. More and more the city was coming to depend on the favor and protection of Rome. After 168 B.C., when the power of Macedon was finally broken

by the Roman victory at Pydna, Athens enjoyed a long period of peace, with great financial prosperity, but her political life was under
control of an aristocracy of the wealthy, supported by Roman over-lords. Finally, early in
the last century before Christ (89–88), a
democratic reaction, led by most incompetent
citizens, involving the attempt to exchange the
support of Rome for that of Mithridates, resulted in a terrible siege by Sulla, and the final
extinction of all democratic institutions. In this
century least of all was there any place for the
influence of the Demosthenic political traditions.

If the practical oratory of the bema and the
courts did little to perpetuate the Demosthenic
traditions of public speech, the leading rhetorical schools of the third and second centuries
before Christ did little more. The Aristotelian
rhetoric, contemporary with Demosthenes, had
ignored him. The Gorgian-Isocratic school
found its models in those masters. The two traditions were carried on as parallel influences in
education; neither of the two looked to the
oratory of Demosthenes for models either of
argumentation or of expression. And yet for a
time at least in the third century there must

have been teachers of rhetoric who were sending their pupils to the speeches of Demosthenes
for study and imitation. We read of a treatise
by Cleochares, in which he maintained the supremacy of Demosthenes as compared with
Isocrates; and more important testimony is the
fact that in the early collections of the speeches
of Demosthenes a considerable number are
found which we now recognize as students' exercises composed in imitation of genuine
speeches of Demosthenes.

When in the course of the third century B.C.
the more popular schools of rhetorical teaching
passed from Athens to Rhodes and the Hellenistic cities of Asia Minor, a new type of
oratory was developed, which had little in common with that of Demosthenes. The so-called
' Asian ' rhetoric was an outgrowth of the Gorgian-Isocratic school, but with all the characteristics of the vitiated literary taste of the age.
There was a manifest attempt at emotional expression with flowery adornment, far-fetched
metaphors, brilliant conceits. The stately Isocratic periods and the nervous and overwhelming periods of Demosthenes were alike abandoned for a style in which short, sharp clauses,
strung one after another, tickled the ear and

gave an almost poetic movement. This Asian school was so popular that during the second half of the third century, and nearly all of the second, the oratory of Demosthenes must have been neglected by most of the schools.

About the middle of the second century B.C. a new movement in rhetoric began under Hermagoras of Tarsus. Hermagoras combined the Aristotelian rhetoric, in which the emphasis was upon the principles of argumentation, with the Gorgian-Isocratic tradition, concerned chiefly with the art of expression. His system became the dominant one in the early Roman period. It can hardly have given much place to the oratory of Demosthenes, but it did tend to send students back to the published works of some of the Attic orators, and we soon find a new tendency in the schools, known as the 'Atticist' movement. Both in Athens and in Rhodes by the end of the second century B.C. some of the teachers were beginning to look to the great Attic orators of the fourth century for their models of style. In the teaching of most of these men Hyperides seems to have held first place, but there were some of these Atticists who preferred Demosthenes and kept alive the enthusiasm for his works. We hear of an orator and rhetorician, Menedemus, active at Athens in the first century B.C., who, in a discussion as to the relation of philosophy to oratory, recited from memory whole passages from Demosthenes. Cicero also tells us of one Pammenes at Athens, the most eloquent speaker there in his time, who was an ardent student of the oratory of Demosthenes and who became the teacher of Brutus.

The study of Greek rhetoric and oratory by the Romans was well established early in the second century B.C., and the popularity of such courses increased rapidly, receiving new impetus by the coming of throngs of Greek teachers after the Roman conquest of Macedon in 168 B.C. The elder Cato, turning late in life to Greek literature, is said to have been especially influenced by the oratory of Demosthenes. By the close of the second century Greek rhetoric was becoming an important factor in the training of those young Romans who were ambitious for a career in politics. Many resorted to the schools of Athens, Rhodes, and the cities of Asiatic Greece. Roman officials in the East welcomed the opportunity to hear courses of lectures by Greek rhetoricians, and there were always teachers of Greek rhetoric in Rome itself. The Asian type of oratory held first place in the earlier years, and was made exceedingly popular in Rome by Hortensius early in the first century B.C. But before the middle of that century the Atticist movement became powerful there, bringing its exaltation of Hyperides and Lysias, or in some cases Thucydides, and even Xenophon. While Demosthenes was not a favorite with the men of this school, so prominent a pleader as Calvus is said to have included his speeches among his own models.

It remained for Cicero to bring the oratory of Demosthenes to full recognition among the Romans. Cicero, entirely familiar with the Greek language, made the study of Greek oratory, during his residence in Athens, Rhodes, and the cities of Asia Minor, a large part of his preparation for public life. His own tastes inclined him toward the showy, Asian style, and he never entirely threw off its influence, but in theory he was convinced of its errors, and he became strongly influenced by the more restrained Rhodian school; and finally in his treatises on the history and theory of oratory he consistently gave to Demosthenes the first place.

"It is astonishing," says Cicero, "how one

among the Greek orators excels all the rest."
Demosthenes is *facile princeps* among the Attic
orators. "His excellence is extraordinary." He
alone corresponds to Cicero's ideal of eloquence. Cicero insinuates that the reason that
the Atticists do not make Demosthenes their
model is that they despair of being able themselves to imitate him. His diction is "perfected
and refined." Greater eloquence than that of
the speech *On the Crown* no man could ask
for. A translation of the speeches of Aeschines
and Demosthenes in the case *On the Crown,*
with an elaborate introduction, was one of
Cicero's mature works.[15]

Cicero nowhere gives a systematic review of
Demosthenes' oratory, but here and there he
mentions specific qualities of it. In a general
characterization of five Attic orators, he as-
cribes to Demosthenes 'force' (*vis*) as compared with the 'sweetness' of Isocrates, the
'simplicity' (*subtilitas*) of Lysias, the 'subtlety' (*acumen*) of Hyperides, and the 'sono-
rousness' of Aeschines. But Cicero fully recognizes the variety which marks Demosthenes'
style. "Demosthenes," he says (*Orator,* 31.
110), "yields in no wise to Lysias in simplicity,
to Hyperides in subtlety and keenness, nor to

Aeschines in rapidity and brilliancy of diction."
Many speeches of Demosthenes are simple
throughout, the speech *Against Leptines* for
example; many are in the 'grand style'
(*graves*) throughout, like some of the *Philippics;* many are diversified, like the speech
against Aeschines *On the Embassy,* and the
speech *For Ctesiphon.* Cicero recognizes the
superiority of Demosthenes in the "ornamentation and arrangement of the thought;" again
he speaks of his very abundant use of the
'figures of thought;' he considers Demosthenes clever rather than witty (*non tam dicax
fuit quam facetus*).

Cicero has observed that Demosthenes in
general avoids hiatus, but he has not seen
wherein he differs in this matter from Isocrates.
Of Demosthenes' rhythmical effects Cicero
says: "Those thunderbolts of his had not so
flashed had they not been borne on with all the
energy of rhythm." But there is nothing to
show that Cicero had so minutely analyzed the
language of Demosthenes as to understand the
secret of his rhythmical effects.

Despite his recognition of the supremacy of
Demosthenes in every type of oratory, Cicero
confesses (*Orator,* 30.104) that he is not quite

satisfied; Demosthenes does not always fill his ears, " so greedy and insatiate are they, always longing for something vast and infinite." It is this confession which gives the clue to the surprising fact that while in his appreciations and criticisms of the Greek orators Cicero repeatedly gives the first place to Demosthenes, in his own highest flights of oratory he comes very much nearer to the type of Isocrates. He praises Demosthenes, but imitates Isocrates. It is just that sonorous balancing of clauses, that fullness of ornament, that amplification of the thought, so characteristic of Isocrates, which Cicero misses in Demosthenes, and which so appeals to his own love of display that it in fact shapes his own style. He did feel to the full the power (*vis*) of Demosthenes' oratory, but he failed to analyze the sources of it. He did not realize that it was powerful just because the orator was intent on one thing only, the clear, sharp expression of a thought that had complete possession of his own mind. Demosthenes did, indeed, use all the devices of artificial rhetoric, and in their proper place all its embellishments, but only as instruments, never as ornaments for display. He did, indeed, often make use of massive periods, but it was a tremendous thought which filled them, not the padding and amplifying of self-conscious exhibition.

The permanent influence of Cicero on the Demosthenic tradition has therefore been anomalous. Wherever in Roman, mediaeval, and modern times Cicero's treatises on the history and theory of oratory have been studied, Demosthenes has been introduced as the supreme orator, his style commended as the norm. But every page of Cicero's own speeches has contributed rather to the perpetuation of the Gorgian-Isocratic type, and his oratory has had an enormous influence in carrying on this type in English and American oratory almost to our own day.

We have in the anonymous rhetorical treatise *Ad Herennium* a Latin work of the same period with Cicero's youthful work *De Inventione*, and going back to the same Greek sources. It is interesting to find that this writer, who composes for himself examples of the various ' figures ' of rhetoric, models a considerable number of them on passages from Demosthenes, while he seems to have used only a single passage of any other Greek orator.

Thirteen years after the death of Cicero a Greek rhetorician and critic, Dionysius of Halicarnassus, took up his residence in Rome. Dionysius was as ardent an admirer of Demosthenes as Cicero had been, and he brought to his lectures and critical essays a more minute study of the technique of style, together with a wide and appreciative knowledge of the Attic writers both in prose and poetry. He lived at Rome for at least twenty-two years, and was constantly teaching and writing, a leader in the campaign of the Atticists against the Asian school, and always exalting Demosthenes as the chief of Attic orators. A considerable part of his work has come down to us. We have a treatise on *Literary Composition,* parts of a critical examination of six of the Attic orators, studies in the styles of Plato and of Thucydides, a careful review of the works of Dinarchus, and an essay proving that the style of Demosthenes was shaped before the publication of Aristotle's *Rhetoric.* Again and again in his essays Dionysius pays supreme tribute to Demosthenes. He says: " When I take in my hands a speech of Demosthenes, I am carried hither and thither; I pass from one emotion to another, doubting, struggling, fearing, despising, hating, pitying; friendly, angry, jealous, possessed by all the feelings to which human nature is subject." (*Demos.*, § 22) Demosthenes, says Dionysius, was not an imitator of any man, but "he selected from the style of each those elements that were strongest and most serviceable. And so he wove a style of his own, one style from many, — elevated and simple; distinguished, plain; unusual, familiar; panegyrical, straightforward; austere, joyous; condensed, unconstrained; sweet, bitter; now revealing character, now expressing emotion. A veritable Proteus as described in the ancient poets, assuming any and every form at will." (*Demos.*, § 8) "Power" ($\delta\epsilon\iota\nu\acute{o}\tau\eta s$) is the distinguishing mark of the oratory of Demosthenes. Its sources are energy, weight, passion, vehemence, vigor. But there is an ever changing variety. Some of his periods are rounded and climactic, others are flowing and diffuse; the length of some falls within a single breath of a speaker, some are four times that length. The rhetorical 'figures' are now those of the austere style, now those which belong to the smooth and flowing type. While the prose rhythms of Demosthenes are usually of the stronger, more masculine movements, the smoother and more musical are not wanting. He has a fine sense of appropriateness — adapting the style to the nature of the subject, and varying it with the demands of the different parts of a speech. In proem and narrative Demosthenes vies with Lysias in sweetness and grace; when he proceeds to argumentation and appeal to the feelings, he has an intensity and strength which are not found in Lysias. Dionysius goes into minute detail in the analysis of the rhythmical movements in Demosthenes' prose. He finds constant use of rhythm, but its various forms so intermingled and so constantly changing that the hearer is in no danger of feeling that the speaker is overstepping the limits of prose. Even as Demosthenes surpasses all his predecessors and his contemporaries, so, in the opinion of Dionysius, he defies the rivalry of the ages.

The generation of young Romans who followed Cicero found all the weight of his authority thrown toward the study of Demosthenes' speeches as the norm in oratory. Dionysius added to this influence his own enthusiasm and his intelligent and minute analysis of the sources of Demosthenes' power. Strangely enough he nowhere, at least in his extant works, makes any comparison between the oratory of the great Athenian and that of Cicero.

Atticists before Dionysius had been inclined each to select some one Attic prose writer as a model for imitation. It was the great merit of Dionysius that he had the critical acumen to discern the elements of permanent value in the style of each of the masters, and to see that the supremacy of Demosthenes lay in his ability to adapt these several types of speech and to combine them into one powerful, varied, comprehensive style. The effect of this was to turn the especial attention of students of rhetoric to Demosthenes, as the man in whose works all the elements of great oratory were to be found.

A contemporary and friend of Dionysius was the Sicilian rhetorician Caecilius of Calacté. In a long residence at Rome Caecilius threw the whole influence of his learning and critical ability to the side of the Atticists. None of his works have come down to us. Among them perhaps the most important was a treatise on the *Ten Attic Orators* — the first reference which we have to the canon of the "Ten." There was also an essay on *Elevation of Style* (Περὶ Ὕψους), and we hear of essays on Antiphon and Lysias, and of comparisons between the oratory of Cicero and that of Demosthenes and Aeschines. Caecilius was an admirer of Lysias; how he ranked him in comparison with Demosthenes we do not know, but he certainly gave Demosthenes a prominent place.

We have in incomplete form another critical essay on *Elevation of Style* (Περὶ Ὕψους, *De Sublimitate*), probably inspired by the essay of Caecilius and written not long after. The author is unknown, but he shows a keen appreciation of style, and his work must have had a fine influence in his own time.[16] The Greeks quoted oftenest in the essay are Homer, Herodotus, Plato, and Demosthenes. The author's comparison between Demosthenes and Cicero is as discerning as it is famous: " Demosthenes is characterized by sublimity which is for the most part rugged, Cicero by profusion. Our orator (Demosthenes) owing to the fact that in his vehemence, — aye, and in his speed, power and intensity, — he can as it were consume by fire and carry away all before him, may be compared to a thunderbolt or flash of lightning. Cicero, on the other hand, it seems to me, after the manner of a wide-spreading conflagration, rolls on with all-devouring flames, having within him an ample and abid-

ing store of fire, distributed now at this point
now at that, and fed by an unceasing succession. . . . The great opportunity of Demosthenes' high-pitched elevation comes where intense utterance and vehement passion are in
question, and in passages in which the audience
is to be utterly enthralled. The profusion of
Cicero is in place where the hearer must be
flooded with words, for it is appropriate to
treatment of commonplaces (τοπηγορίαι),
and to perorations for the most part and digres-
sions, and to all descriptive and declamatory
passages, and to writings on history and natural science, and to many other departments of
literature." (XII. 4 f., W. Rhys Roberts' translation.)

Of the " Marathonian Oath," in the climax
of the *Crown Speech*, he says: " In the public
view by this one Figure of Adjuration, which
I here term *Apostrophe*, he deifies his ancestors. He brings home the thought that we ought
to swear by those who have thus nobly died
as we swear by Gods, and he fills the minds of
the judges with the high spirit of those who
there bore the brunt of the danger, and he has
transformed the natural course of the argument into transcendent sublimity and passion

and that secure belief which rests upon strange and prodigious oaths. He instils into the minds of his hearers the conviction — which acts as a medicine and an antidote — that they should, uplifted by these eulogies, feel no less proud of the fight against Philip than of the triumph at Marathon and Salamis. By all these means he carries his hearers clean away with him through the employment of a single figure. . . . The oath is framed for vanquished men, with the intention that Chaeronea should no longer appear a failure to the Athenians." (XVI. 2 f., Roberts' trans.)

A treatise which has come down to us under the title *Demetrius on Style* (Δημητρίου περὶ Ἑρμηνείας) probably belongs to the time of Cicero or to that of Dionysius of Halicarnassus.[17] The (unknown) author has not the command of the minutiae of rhetorical theory which we find in Dionysius, and in literary appreciation he is not to be compared with the author of the essay on *Elevation of Style;* but he is a fairly competent student of literature and composition. It is significant that in his quotations from Attic orators Demosthenes is the favorite. Hyperides is not cited, Aeschines only twice, Isocrates and Lysias three times each, while thirteen passages from De-mosthenes are quoted, — these for the most part in illustrating the quality of force (δεινότης).

In the *Dialogus de Oratoribus*, belonging to the last quarter of the first century A.D., and attributed to Tacitus, Demosthenes is spoken of as generally recognized as standing at the head of the Attic orators; in the next rank are Aeschines, Hyperides, Lysias, and Lycur-gus (Chapter 25). In another passage the fame of Homer is likened to that of Demos-thenes, the fame of Sophocles and Euripides to that of Lysias and Hyperides (Chapter 12).

Finally, in the closing years of the first cen-tury A.D., the publication of Quintilian's *Insti-tutio Oratoria* gave a verdict on the place of Demosthenes among the Attic orators which became definitive for Roman students of rheto-ric. Quintilian gives to Demosthenes among the Greeks and Cicero among the Romans a place of unapproachable supremacy. While he no-where makes any such minute study of the style of Demosthenes as that which we have in Dionysius, he gives more than one summary appreciation, and shows his entire accord with the conclusions of Cicero and Dionysius. Quintilian regards Cicero as in some respects a greater orator than Demosthenes, for he says that Cicero "succeeded in reproducing the force of Demosthenes, the copious flow of Plato, and the charm of Isocrates" (X. 1. 108). In the tenth book of the *Institutes* he sums up his estimate of the two orators in these words: "But it is our orators, above all, who enable us to match our Roman eloquence against that of Greece. For I would set Cicero against any one of their orators without fear of refutation. I know well enough what a storm I shall raise by this assertion, more especially since I do not propose for the moment to compare him with Demosthenes; for there could be no point in such a comparison, as I consider that Demosthenes should be the object of special study, and not merely studied, but even committed to memory. I regard the excellence of these two orators as being for the most part similar, that is to say, their judgment, their gift of arrangement, their methods of division, preparation and proof, as well as everything concerned with invention. In their actual style there is some difference. Demosthenes is more concentrated, Cicero more diffuse; Demosthenes makes his periods shorter than Cicero, and his weapon is the rapier, whereas Cicero's periods are longer, and at times he employs the bludgeon as well: nothing can be taken from the former, nor added to the latter; the Greek reveals a more studied, the Roman a more natural art." (X. 1.105 ff., Butler's translation in *The Loeb Classical Library*). Again he says: *Longe princeps Demosthenes ac paene lex orandi fuit.* (X. 1. 76.)

While the study of rhetoric and oratory had become fully at home in Rome from the time of Cicero onward, yet its chief centers were the Greek cities themselves, Athens long holding the first place. A considerable number of Greek treatises on rhetoric have come down to us from the second and third centuries A.D. It is significant that in these Demosthenes holds the unquestioned primacy. So far as these teachers of rhetoric illustrate their definitions and theories by quotations from the orators, they all depend chiefly upon Demosthenes; some of them cite him exclusively. There is apparently no longer any such rivalry of claims between admirers of Lysias, Hyperides, or Isocrates, as we find in the time of Cicero or of Dionysius. References to any orator save Demosthenes are now exceptional.

Aelius Aristides, orator and rhetorician, trained at Pergamum and Athens, was in his own time, the second century, most popular. In his speeches he was a professed imitator of the style of Demosthenes.[18]

An *Encomium on Demosthenes,* a little treatise which has come down with the works of Lucian, is in the form of a dialogue, in which the writer, as in the person of the Macedonian Antipater himself, expresses his admiration for the incorruptible patriotism of Demosthenes, his watchfulness, his efficiency, his untiring labors. Testimony to the oratorical power of Demosthenes shows that the writer, like Demosthenes' most ardent admirers, regards him as holding the place among orators which Homer holds among the poets.[19]

Hermogenes of Tarsus, active in the later years of the second century and the early years of the third, was the author of a *Compendium of Rhetoric,* which became a standard among the schools of the later classic period and throughout Byzantine times, holding much the same place among Greek treatises which Quintilian's *Institutes* held among the Latin. Hermogenes was not a gifted critic like Caecilius or Dionysius, but he had a comprehensive knowledge of rhetorical theory, and he was an ardent student of Attic oratory. He had edited some at least of the speeches of Demosthenes. With considerable skill and good judgment Hermogenes fashioned from the works of his predecessors an eclectic system, very full in detail, simple and clear in definition, an available text-book for the schools. For the student of Demosthenic tradition the fact of especial interest in the work of Hermogenes is that in his view Demosthenes is the commanding orator; indeed he often speaks of him simply as " The Orator." Hermogenes makes constant use of quotations to illustrate his rhetorical definitions, and in almost all cases these illustrations are taken from the speeches of Demosthenes.[20] In fact the *Rhetoric* of Hermogenes might almost be called a rhetorical commentary on the speeches of Demosthenes. Even in cases where Lysias or another Greek orator might be considered the typical representative of the style under discussion, Hermogenes goes to Demosthenes for his illustrations. The great popularity of the *Rhetoric* of Hermogenes in the succeeding centuries — volumes of commentaries were written to expound its teachings

— tended to foster the interest in Demosthenes himself and to incite students to read his speeches.[21]

And yet dominant as the oratory of Demosthenes had become in the theories of the schools, the practical oratory of the second and third centuries was shaped by a very different influence, a revived Asianism, with all its extravagance of ornament, its artificial devices, its brilliance of diction covering dullness of thought. And this is not strange. The current rhetoric was not perpetuating those features of the Demosthenic oratory which gave it its real power, but only its more artificial features, its tricks of argumentation, its superficial ornaments. The rhetoricians of these times had no real grasp of the sources of his power, such understanding as we find in Cicero and Dionysius. They became, therefore, in spite of their constant citations of Demosthenes, the teachers of a very different type of public speech, the natural outgrowth of the circumstances of their own time. For the second century A.D. saw the beginning of a brilliant epoch in the inner life of the Greek cities. Protected by the Romans and not seriously exploited by them, the Greek cities received in compensation for the loss of their political freedom a wide field for commercial enterprise, and under Hadrian and the Antonines they enjoyed the imperial bounty in everything which tended to develop their artistic and literary life. Costly public buildings were erected by the Emperors, the national games were restored to their old splendor, the Emperors themselves made brilliant tours from city to city, everywhere appearing as the patrons of art and letters. In the field of literature, rhetoric now took the commanding place — almost the exclusive place. Philosophy, once the mistress of the Greek schools, had to yield now to oratory. Chairs of Rhetoric were established by the Emperors not only in Rome, but in more than one of the Greek cities. Athens became the center of Greek rhetorical studies in the West, Smyrna in the East. In many a Greek city the professor of Rhetoric came to be regarded as the leading citizen. He it was who welcomed the Emperor or the high Roman official on his arrival at the gates of the town; his epideictic speech of welcome and compliment was the event of the year. Greek rhetoricians were rewarded with important appointments at the Imperial court; sons of royalty were among their young pupils, sometimes the

Emperor himself was an auditor in the lecture-room. In his home town the rhetorician held high office; no other was so eligible as he for a diplomatic mission; no one oftener received the honor of a complimentary vote of the people, or a statue erected by a grateful state; and when he went abroad on a professional tour, crowds in every city flocked to hear his advertised ' oration,' a speech which was, according to the ideals of the time, a masterpiece of ' art for art's sake.'

The second and third centuries, therefore, while in theory doing homage to Demosthenes, and, indeed, borrowing the more superficial ornaments of his style, had no sympathy with the spirit which gave to his oratory its essential power, and no deep appreciation of his eloquence. The passionate, serious eloquence of his best harangues was as far as possible from the smooth and elegant style of the day, a style which was in fact a corrupted inheritance from Gorgias and Isocrates.

With the transfer of the Imperial court to Constantinople in 330 A.D. that city became a center of Greek influence in rhetoric and oratory. Athens meanwhile retained her prominence as a seat of rhetorical studies, and for a time Antioch was the home of another influential school.

To this period of the increasing influence of the Greek cities of the East belongs Libanius the Sophist (314–393 A.D.), student of rhetoric at Athens, teacher of rhetoric for a time at Constantinople and Nicomedia, and for the remainder of his long life at his boyhood home, Antioch in Syria. Libanius was both teacher of rhetoric and popular orator, the most popular of his generation, friend of successive emperors, and teacher of Johannes Chrysostom, the most eloquent of the Greek church fathers. Now to Libanius the oratory of Demosthenes was the chief object of study and emulation. He, therefore, more than any other man, carried the Demosthenic tradition over into the Byzantine period, and through his greatest pupil gave to it an early influence on the Christian pulpit.

The two other most famous preachers of the fourth century (the greatest century in Greek pulpit eloquence), Basil the Great and Gregory of Nazianzus, were trained in rhetoric at Athens under Himerius, a teacher who, if not a profound student of Demosthenes, certainly made some use of him.

Little has come down to us from the rhetorical studies of the fourth and fifth centuries. The elementary text-book of Aphthonius of Antioch had very great influence in later times, but it makes no use of illustrations from the orators. We have several commentaries on Hermogenes from this period, and in them we find many references to Demosthenes, few to the other orators; evidently the tradition of his superiority was fully maintained.

While the critics and rhetoricians like Cicero, Dionysius, Quintilian and their successors had been steadily exalting Demosthenes to the first place among Greek orators, a body of practical helps to the study of Demosthenes in the schools had been growing up. A *Lexicon of the Ten Orators,* by Harpocration of Alexandria (of uncertain date), supplied valuable information, especially as to antiquities and proper names. By the second century we find traces of commentaries on Demosthenes which analyzed his style, showing its varied features (ἰδέαι) and treating his speeches as the models of political oratory and as the embodiment of " mastery " in speech (δεινότης).[22] " Introductions " to the several speeches were prepared by Libanius, and these have been preserved in the manuscripts of the speeches. "Notes" on the speeches were all the time accumulating; many of these appear on the margins of our manuscripts. About the beginning of the second century Plutarch's biography of Demosthenes in the *Parallel Lives* gathered together, if in an uncritical way, yet in an attractive and vivid form, the biographical material which had been handed down in the five centuries which had passed since the death of the orator. Later than Plutarch appeared an anonymous book, *The Lives of the Ten Orators,* including a life of Demosthenes, in which fact and legend are hopelessly mingled. Other "lives" followed, by Libanius in the fourth century, by Zosimus a century and a half later; another anonymous life was written later still.[23]

With the coming of the northern barbarians into Italy, and the decay of the Roman culture, Constantinople and the other Greek cities of the East took on new importance as centers of Greek learning. The influence of the Christian pulpit tended to perpetuate the Greek rhetoric, and this carried with it the continued study of the Greek orators. In the long period from the sixth century to the fourteenth there was probably no generation in which some men of the Greek schools were not reading Demosthenes, though possibly at times only in books of extracts or compendiums of literature. In the revival of the study of the classic authors which began in the Greek East in the ninth century the works of Demosthenes certainly found a place. Photius gives to him full recognition in his sketch of the surviving Greek authors. The popularity of the rhetoric of Hermogenes in the Byzantine schools tended to keep alive the interest in Demosthenes, the orator on whose works this rhetoric was founded. While the Byzantine scholars made no important contributions to the literature of Demosthenes, they did keep alive the traditions, and they preserved the manuscripts, so that when in the fourteenth and fifteenth centuries the call came from Europe for the restoration of the long lost speeches, the Byzantine teachers were ready with manuscripts and commentaries. We have from the ninth to the eleventh centuries three manuscripts of Demosthenes which are nearly complete, and five others which contain considerable parts of his speeches, a manuscript tradition much more extensive than that of any other Greek orator.[24]

IV. DEMOSTHENES IN MODERN EUROPE

THE study of Demosthenes in the western world of the Renaissance began with the lectures of Chrysoloras, a Greek scholar who came to Italy from Constantinople in 1396, and taught in Florence, Venice, Padua, Milan, and Rome. He was the first professor of Greek in the West, the first to lecture on Demosthenes, and perhaps the first to bring a manuscript of the speeches from the East. His transcript of the Greek text is in the Vatican, and we have a letter of his on the meaning of technical terms involved in certain of the speeches.

In 1423 nearly all the speeches of Demosthenes came to Italy among the 238 Greek manuscripts brought over by Aurispa. Leonardo Bruni (1369–1444), a pupil of Chrysoloras at Florence, translated into Latin Demosthenes' *Third Olynthiac*, the speech *On the Chersonese*, and the speeches of Demosthenes and Aeschines *On the Crown*. This Latin version of the two speeches *On the Crown* was printed in Venice in 1485. In the middle of the fifteenth century Vittorino established at Mantua the first great humanistic school of Italy. Nowhere in the West at this time was Greek so well taught, and here Demosthenes had a large place in the curriculum, not only with mature students, but with boys and girls as well. " Whole orations of Cicero or Demosthenes, books of Livy and Sallust besides large portions of Virgil and Homer, were recited with accuracy and taste by boys or girls of less than fourteen years of age." [25]

In the middle of the century Theodorus Gaza, a Greek from Thessalonica and the ablest classical scholar of his time, was lecturing on Demosthenes at Ferrara, and in the last quarter of the century Janus Lascaris, a Greek from Constantinople, was lecturing at Florence on the same orator.

When in the last quarter of that century the Turks were pressing upon Christendom, Bessarion, Patriarch of Constantinople, earnestly giving himself to the attempt to unite the Eastern and Western churches, used as a part of his propaganda for union against the barbarians a Latin translation of the *First Olynthiac,* which he had caused to be printed at Paris. In his comments on the ancient fight for freedom Bessarion summoned the Christian princes to the impending struggle.

In France, England, and Germany Greek studies were making their way very slowly. Individual students from those countries were studying in Italy, and were bringing back Greek manuscripts. Many other Greek manuscripts were brought directly from the Greek cities, and were widely copied; and certain wandering Greeks were giving something of Greek instruction, but we have no mention of the teaching of Demosthenes until late in this century.

The *Editio Princeps* of the Greek text of Demosthenes came from the press of Aldus Manutius at Venice in 1504. This text, based on three Greek manuscripts, was the joint work of Aldus and Scipio Fortiguerra (Carteromachos), Secretary of the New Academy of Hellenists. The volume contained all the speeches ascribed by manuscript tradition to Demosthenes, the Introductions and ' Life ' by Libanius, the ' Life ' by Plutarch, and an index of variant readings.

In 1543 another complete and carefully

edited edition of the speeches was published in Venice by Felicianus. Between 1550 and 1557 Italian scholars published Latin translations of the speeches *On the Peace* and *On the Chersonese,* and translation into Italian was well begun in versions of the *Olynthiacs* and *Philippics,* the speeches *On the Embassy* and *On the Crown,* the *Midiana,* the *Leptinea,* and the speech *Against Androtion.*

Meanwhile the study of Greek had made sufficient progress in Northern Europe to make possible the study of Demosthenes in France, Switzerland, Germany, and England. From the press of the Basel publisher, Johannes Hervagius, a text of all the speeches appeared in 1532, and to the Lives and Introductions were added Ulpian's *Scholia* and notes from the studies of Erasmus, Budaeus, and others, with a table of variant readings. Erasmus contributed a preface to this volume. French scholarship was represented by the edition of Benenatus, Paris, 1570.

In 1572 the publication at Basel of the great edition of Hieronymus Wolf of Augsburg marked a new stage in the study of Demosthenes. Wolf had published a complete Latin translation of the speeches twenty-two years earlier; he now added to this a revised Greek text, and with the Lives and Introductions, together with ancient and modern notes and variant readings, he gave to the student a generous apparatus for Demosthenic studies. In the volume he included the speeches of Aeschines, in Greek and Latin.

In Germany the study of Demosthenes was already flourishing before the publication of Wolf's great Graeco-Latin edition. In the last quarter of the fifteenth century Reuchlin, one of the "two eyes" of humanistic Germany, was lecturing on Demosthenes, and the earliest definitely dated German translation of any Greek work is a German version of the *First Olynthiac,* which Reuchlin sent in manuscript to Count Eberhard of Würtemberg, who was then attending the famous Diet of Worms of 1495. Some have thought that in the mind of Reuchlin the Demosthenic summons was to the Emperor Maximilian to resist the pretensions of the French Emperor. Reuchlin translated also the *First* and *Second Philippics,* and one of the last acts of his life was to urge the hasty printing of an edition of Demosthenes and Aeschines *On the Crown,* to be used by his students at Tübingen. The volume came from the press in 1521, after Reuchlin's death, and was the first edition of the great speech to be printed separately. Reuchlin passed on the Demosthenic tradition to his nephew, Philip Melanchthon, scholar of the German Reformation. Melanchthon began the publication of Latin translations in 1524 with the *First Olynthiac*. The other *Olynthiacs* and the *First Philippic* followed, and the speech *Against Aristogiton* was added. These translations were again and again reprinted, two of them fourteen times. His Latin translation of Aeschines and Demosthenes *On the Crown* was printed in 1562, two years after his death. In his introduction to the *First Olynthiac*, Melanchthon says we cannot hope for a translation which shall completely reproduce the combined strength and beauty of this surpassing oratory until Nature shall have produced another Demosthenes. In the speech *Against Aristogiton* Demosthenes describes the defendant as a man who creeps through the Agora like a viper or a scorpion with uplifted sting, a man without friends or associates, his only companions those whom the painters portray as attending the wicked in Hades — Malediction, Defamation, Envy, Discord, Strife. Of this tremendous indictment Melanchthon says: "No writer of tragedy was ever able to say anything more brilliant." Melanchthon closes the introduction to the same speech with words which show how far he was from thinking of studies in Demosthenes as purely linguistic or literary: "Would that there were no Aristogitons in the States of today! But whereas at Athens there was one solitary Aristogiton, now many are in power everywhere, and worse they are than Aristogiton of Athens, in that they cloak private greed with the pretext of religion. When their image shall be seen depicted here, may good youths perceive therein an admonition to themselves, that they may study to show themselves better men than they, and to bring modesty and other virtues to the service of the State."

While Melanchthon was spreading the knowledge of Demosthenes throughout Germany by his Latin translations of the speeches, the other maker of the school system of Protestant Germany, Johannes Sturm, was giving the study of Cicero and Demosthenes the central place in the curriculum of the new Gymnasium at Strassburg. The study of Cicero was a part of the course from the very first reading in Latin to the beginning of professional studies, and in the higher classes Demosthenes had an important place. Even in his student days in Paris, Sturm had been lecturing, as privat docent, on Demosthenes, and the very great emphasis which he always placed on the study of ancient rhetoric as embodied in classical oratory gave impetus to Demosthenic studies.

In the sixteenth century we hear of only one translation of the speeches of Demosthenes into German, a version of the four *Philippics*, made from the Latin, and published at Augsburg in 1543.

The first translation of Demosthenes into the French language was that of the three *Olynthiacs* by Louis Le Roy, Paris, 1541. Guillaume du Vair, ecclesiastic and publicist, added to his treatise on French eloquence (1592–93) a French translation of Demosthenes' and Aeschines' speeches *On the Crown*. A half-dozen other French translations of selected speeches of Demosthenes appeared before the close of the sixteenth century.

We know that the study of Greek began in England soon after the middle of the fifteenth century, but it is doubtful whether anything of Demosthenes was read in this earliest period.

Individual Englishmen may have learned something of his oratory in their studies in Italy. But in 1540 Sir John Cheke became first Regius Professor of Greek at Cambridge, and afterward Public Orator of the University. Shortly after Cheke's appointment, Roger Ascham in a private letter, writing of the progress of Greek studies in St. John's College, says, probably with something of exaggeration, that now Demosthenes is as well known there as Cicero was at an earlier time. We have the testimony of Thomas Wylson, the first English translator of Demosthenes, to Cheke's devotion to the orator. Wylson, in the introductory epistle of his translation, speaks of Cheke as having " traveled in Demosthenes as much as any one of them all," and he recalls his own experience at Padua, when all the English students there were inspired by Cheke " to go to their booke," and he tells us how Cheke read gladly to himself and others certain orations of Demosthenes in Greek, and interpreted them. Of Cheke's command of Demosthenes he says: " Such acquaintance had he with this notable orator, so gladly did he read him, and so often: that I thinke there was neuer olde Priest more perfite in his Portreise, nor supersticious

Monke in our Ladies Psalter as they call it, nor yet good preacher in the Bible or testament, than this man was in Demosthenes. . . . He was moued greatly to like Demosthenes aboue all others, for that he saw him so familiarly applying himselfe to the sense and vnderstanding of the common people, that he sticked not to say, that none euer was more fitte to make an English man tell his tale praise worthily in an open hearing, either in Parlament or in Pulpit, or otherwise, than this onely orator was." Among the works of Cheke were Latin translations of the *Philippics* and *Olynthiacs*, together with the *Leptinea* and "the orations of Demosthenes and Aeschines on the two opposite sides."

Roger Ascham says in the *Scholemaster:* " Yea, I haue heard worthie M. Cheke many tymes say: I would haue a good student passe and journey through all authors both Greeke and Latin: but he that will dwell in these few bookes onelie: first, in Gods holie Bible, and then ioyne with it, *Tullie* in *Latin, Plato, Aristotle: Xenophon: Isocrates:* and *Demosthenes* in Greeke: must nedes proue an excellent man." Ascham further says that Redman, Cheke, Smith, and their scholars brought Aris-

[140]

totle, Plato, Cicero, and Demosthenes "to florishe as notable in Cambridge, as euer they did in Grece and in Italie: and for the doctrine of those fowre, the fowre pillars of learning, Cambridge then geuing place to no vniuersitie, neither in France, Spaine, Germanie, nor Italie."

Ascham, who calls Sir John Cheke "my dearest frend, and teacher of all the little poor learning I haue," had the privilege of bringing Demosthenes to Queen Elizabeth herself. Her tutor before her accession to the throne and director of her studies afterward, he tells us how, after a dinner at Windsor Castle, where the discussion had turned on school discipline, he "went vp to read with the Queenes Maiestie. We red then togither in the Greke tonge as I well remember, that noble oration of Demosthenes against Aeschines for his false dealing in his ambassage to king Philip of Macedonie." In the *Scholemaster* he tells of the progress in Greek which Elizabeth has made by daily exercise for a year or two in 'double translation' from Isocrates and Demosthenes. For perfecting style he gives this advice: "If a Master woulde haue a perfite example to folow, how, in *Genere sublimi,* to auoide *Nimium,* or in

Mediocri to atteyne *Satis*, or in *Humili*, to ex-
chew *Parum*, let him read diligently for the
first, *Secundam Philippicam*, for the meane, *De
Natura Deorum*, and for the lowest, *Parti-
tiones*. Or, if in an other tong, ye looke for like
example, in like perfection, for all those three
degrees, read *Pro Ctesiphonte, Ad Leptinem*,
et *Contra Olympiodorum*, and, what witte,
Arte, and diligence is hable to affourde, ye shall
plainely see." He adds that in his opinion no
man of his time is perfect in all three styles
save his friend Iohannes Sturm (the Strassburg student of Cicero and Demosthenes). In
1550 we find Ascham reading Herodotus,
Sophocles, and Demosthenes to Sir Richard
Morisine, whom he was serving as secretary
on an embassy to Germany. Possibly the suggestion which Ascham gives for the improve-
ment of a controversialist of his own day might
not have been without value to certain silver-
tongued men of our own time: "If *Osorius*
would leaue of his lustiness in striuing against
S. Austen, and his ouer rancke rayling against
poore *Luther*, and the troth of Gods doctrine,
and giue his whole studie, not to write any
thing of his own for a while, but to translate
Demosthenes, with so straite, fast, and temper-

ate a style in Latine, as he is in Greeke, he would become so perfit and pure a writer, I beleue, as hath beene fewe or none sence *Ciceroes* dayes: And so, by doing himself and all learned moch good, do others lesse harme, and Christes doctrine lesse injury, than he doth."

At Cambridge, Nicholas Carr, who became Regius Professor of Greek in 1547, carried on the Demosthenic tradition. Francis Bacon says of him that he " almost deified Demosthenes." In 1571 he published a Latin translation of the *Olynthiacs* and *Philippics*.

The first English version of Demosthenes is of peculiar interest, for it is believed to have been made at the solicitation of Queen Elizabeth, at a time when she was facing her desperate struggle against a modern Philip, and had need of every appeal to the English love of liberty. The title-page reads: The three Orations of Demosthenes, chiefe Orator among the Grecians, in fauour of the Olynthians, a people in Thracia, novv called Romania: vvith those his fovver Orations titled expressely & by name against King Philip of Macedonie: most nedefull to be redde in these daungerous dayes, of all them that loue their Countries libertie, and desire to take vvarning for their better auayle, by example of others. Englished out of the Greeke By Thomas Wylson Doctor of the ciuill lavves. After these orations ended, Demosthenes lyfe is set foorth, and gathered out of Plutarch, Lucian, Suidas, and others, with a large table, declaring all the principall matters contayned in euerye part of this booke. Seene and allowed according to the Queenes Maiesties Iniunctions. *Imprinted at London by Henrie Denham.*

The book is dedicated " To the right Honorable Sir William Cecill, Knight, principall Secretarie to the Queens Maiestie." It is to be regretted that English orators of the later period did not profit more by Wylson's comparison of Cicero with Demosthenes: " Demosthenes hath more matter couched in a small roume, than Tullie hath in a large discourse, and Demosthenes writing is more binding, more fast, firme, and more agreable to our common manner of speach, than Tullies Orations are. And who so speaketh now as Demosthenes doth, I doe thynke he should be counted the wiser, the more temperate, and the more graue man a great deale, than if he wholly followed Tullie, and used his large veyne and vehement manner of eloquence." Wylson alludes to the charge

[144]

that Demosthenes was not brave on the battle-field, saying that he " had the stomacke of a Lion, to speake boldly although not to fight manfully." He concludes the *Testimonia* with these words: " Thus much of this worthy and famous Demosthenes, whose name as it is by interpretation the strength and force of the people: so was he in very deede and by nature, the strong bulwarke, and mighty defence of his most deare natiue Countrie."

Wylson's translation was issued in 1570. He had already published his *Rule of Reason, conteyning the Arte of Logike,* and his *Arte of Rheturique.* A member of the inner circle of English Hellenists, student and friend of Cheke, and friend of Ascham, and in his later years holding important civil office, Wylson gave a distinct impulse to the study of Demosthenes in England as bearing on the service of the State.

The seventeenth century saw no new volumes of the Demosthenic corpus, but we find a score of editions of selected speeches, chiefly the *Olynthiacs* and *Philippics,* and the *Crown Speech.* Nearly all of these were by German and French scholars: none were of great importance, and no noteworthy translations into the modern languages were made. It would seem that the great edition of Wolf, reprinted in 1604, 1607, and 1642, met the needs of the more advanced students throughout the century.

The eighteenth century was a time of marked progress both in editing and expounding the text, and in translation. Two great text editions appeared, with introductions, notes and indices: Taylor, Cambridge, 1748–1774, and Reiske, Leipzig, 1770–1775.[26] Some twenty-five editions of selected speeches were published, eleven of them in Great Britain. Translations were numerous, both in Latin and in the modern languages. The English translation of Leland, London, 1756–1777, became a standard; it included the public speeches, and Aeschines and Demosthenes *On the Crown*. Auger's French translation of all the speeches of Aeschines and Demosthenes (1777) was equally valuable. The geographical range of the texts and translations shows how widely the study of Demosthenes was extending in the eighteenth century — from Rome to Moscow, from Paris to Dublin. It is interesting to find among the English editions a translation of the *Second* and *Third Olynthiacs* by the Right Honourable George Granville, written in 1702, the year of his entering Parliament. Johnson says that Granville published this translation " with the design of turning the thunder of Demosthenes upon the head of Lewis."

While much that is best in Demosthenic style is inevitably lost in translation — the emphasis of words and phrases, and the artistic periodic structure — yet the translation when it is well done can bring over much that is characteristic both in thought and expression, and it can reproduce fully the splendid political aims and principles of his career. The widespread translations of the eighteenth century were therefore a powerful means of extending his influence in the States of Europe. Leland writes as follows in his preface: " To animate a public renowned for justice, humanity, and valour, yet in many instances degenerate and corrupted; to warn them of the dangers of luxury, treachery, and bribery, of the ambition of a powerful foreign enemy; to recall the glory of their ancestors to their thoughts and to inspire them with resolution, vigour, and unanimity; to correct abuses, to restore discipline, to revive and enforce the generous sentiments of patriotism and public spirit — these were the great purposes for which the following orations were originally pronounced. The subject therefore may possibly recommend them to a British reader, even under the disadvantages of a translation by no means worthy of the famous original."

Throughout the nineteenth century Demosthenic studies received their full share of the more critical historical and philological investigations, especially in Germany, France, and England. New editions of the whole corpus, based on better knowledge of the whole manuscript tradition, prepared the way for a host of annotated editions of separate speeches. Among the latter, editions of the public speeches by Henri Weil are preëminent. Among the numerous translations, Jacobs' German translation of the *Philippics* (1805) is noteworthy both for the text and the explanatory material. It is interesting to learn that Jacobs in his work, and Niebuhr, then an unknown young man, in a German translation of the *First Philippic* published the year after, both treated Demosthenes' struggle against Philip as a stimulating example to the German peoples in their desperate war with Napoleon. Niebuhr dedicated his little volume to the Czar Alexander, with an adaptation of Virgil's words:

Hic rem Romanam, magno turbante tumultu,
Sistet, eques sternet Poenos Gallumque rebellem.

A translation of the whole corpus by Charles
Rann Kennedy (1848) was of especial value to
English readers.

Comprehensive works on political and legal
antiquities made the speeches more intelligible.
Most important of all were two great works,
Arnold Schaefer's *Demosthenes und seine Zeit,*
and the volume *Demosthenes* in Friedrich
Blass' *Die Attische Beredsamkeit.* Schaefer, in
his three volumes, treats in the utmost detail
every step of Demosthenes' political career,
writing from the standpoint of an outspoken
admirer. Blass, bringing to the study of Demosthenes' speeches a critical knowledge of all
Greek oratory, gives the most minute criticism
of the argument and style of every speech.
Another powerful influence toward the appreciation of Demosthenes came from Grote's *His-*
tory of Greece (1846–1856). Grote, a man
active in the ranks of the extreme Liberals of
his own time, brought to his study of the career
of Demosthenes a profound faith in democracy,
and a real enthusiasm for Demosthenes' struggle
to maintain democracy against the Macedonian

[149]

imperial monarchy. Mitford's *History of Greece*
(1784–1810) had treated the period from the
standpoint of an ultra Tory; Grote carried
English opinion to the opposite view, as Schaefer was doing at the same time in Germany.
Lord Brougham also was lending his great influence to the honor of Demosthenes in his
essays, *Demosthenes, The Eloquence of the
Ancients,* the *Glasgow Inaugural Discourse,* and
his translations of the speeches *On the Chersonese* and *On the Crown.* Brougham, with his
practical experience both in politics and oratory,
made an indispensable addition to the studies of
historians and philologians. But even in a period
in which Demosthenes was so generally admired, occasional protests were made, and very
near the close of the nineteenth century a movement began among some of the ablest German
scholars which at the first threatened Demosthenes' reputation for political sagacity, and
finally would discredit his integrity altogether.
As German scholars looked back upon the
Greek states as they were in the time of Demosthenes, helpless in their separative disorganiza-
tion, and apparently in a position to secure
strength and prosperity by union under the
monarch of Macedon, they could not fail to be

impressed by the analogy of the one-time situation of the states of Germany, at the mercy of
one another and of their powerful neighbors,
until the Prussian monarchs brought them unity
and power. If a Grote and a Brougham saw in
Demosthenes the champion of their own ideal
democracy, certainly men who were enjoying
the marvelous prosperity of imperial Germany
could not fail to see in a Frederick the Great
or a Wilhelm I another Philip of Macedon, and
in the opposition to the Macedonian Empire
they saw only a suicidal attempt to maintain the
system of petty states. Beloch, in Vol. II of his
Griechische Geschichte (1897), so interpreted
the struggle of Demosthenes against Philip.
Eduard Meyer added his commanding influence
to this view, and Paul Wendland followed.[27]
Finally, in 1916, when German imperialism
seemed to be on the point of sweeping French
and English democracy before its resistless military power, Engelbert Drerup, in his little volume, *Aus einer alten Advokatenrepublik*, re-
wrote the story of Demosthenes' public life,
upon the assumption that Demosthenes was a
typical demagogue, with an eye single to his own
advancement, leader of a party 'from the
streets,' and the forerunner of those modern

lawyer-politicians, Asquith, Lloyd George, Poincaré, and their like, who were hastening England and France to their ruin. And now, the World War over, and the modern democracies triumphant, Georges Clemenceau seeks to bring Demosthenes back to his own. In the little volume *Démosthène,* with no pretension to critical study of the sources, in language more dithyrambic than sober, Clemenceau, out of the vicissitudes of his own experience, pays homage to the man who knew how to hold up to its own best ideals a democratic people, fickle in time of peace, gloriously united and heroic in the face of danger.[28]

V. THE INFLUENCE OF DEMOS-
THENES ON ENGLISH AND
AMERICAN ORATORY

WHILE the eighteenth century saw the study of Demosthenes in the Greek well established in all the advanced European countries, it was in Great Britain that it found soil where its fruits could most enrich public life. The growing power of the English Parliament and the rising tide of democracy were developing that parliamentary oratory which was to reach its culmination in the elder Pitt and Edmund Burke. Even in that imperial age there was enough of democratic feeling and of sympathy with the apostles of freedom across the Atlantic to give some real appreciation of the Greek champion of liberty and democracy, while the matured prose composition inherited from the Elizabethan masters needed only the models of Greek and Roman oratory to lift it to the highest plane of eloquence. Cicero and Demosthenes were by this time fully incorporated in the curriculum of school and college.

Eton, the training school of British statesmen,
sent its young men up to Oxford and Cambridge
thoroughly trained in Greek and Latin. Any
young man who aspired to public life had both
motive and opportunity for the extended study
of Greek and Roman oratory in the original
languages. But the effect of such studies in
Cicero and Demosthenes is to be seen not chiefly
in conscious imitation either of thought or
rhetorical structure, but in the standards of
thought and speech unconsciously formed in the
young student, and greatly developed by his
later reading, — for we must remember that the
university graduate of the eighteenth century
did not so often as with us abandon his reading
of the ancient classics on leaving the university.
This classical influence is admirably described
by Erskine in his letter introductory to Wright's
edition of the speeches of Charles James Fox:
" The great orations of antiquity were composed with the utmost labour, were carefully
worked upon and refined by their few great
authors, and pronounced in public after all the
previous study which is necessary to bestow
perfection upon the impassioned declamations
of the stage. But these splendid compositions,
though they have conferred immortal fame upon

eloquence, though they have been the sources of the purest taste, and have given the happiest direction to British genius, have nevertheless produced in England a character of public speaking entirely different, and, in my mind, beyond all comparison superior." The style of English statesmen and lawyers " must not derive its lustre from studied preparation, but from their having worked into their minds from earliest life the great models of taste and genius which, by a kind of human instinct, have united all ages and nations in universal admiration; for the rest, and that by far the most important part of true eloquence, they must trust to the spontaneous, or rather accidental effusions of the divine spirit of man, struck out like fire from its ethereal and immortal nature, when its energies are excited by the great duties which God has imposed upon the few whom he has eminently qualified for the direction and government of mankind."

The first English statesman in whose case we have good reason to infer the influence of Demosthenes is the man whom contemporaries and posterity unite in declaring to be the greatest of the English orators, William Pitt, first Earl of Chatham. Pitt's eight years at Eton and his year at Oxford fell between 1718 and 1727. Tradition says that in his student days he was definitely and persistently training himself for a career as a public speaker, and that Demosthenes, Bolingbroke, and Barrow were his favorite models. We are told that he attributed his ready choice of words to his father's requirement that every day, after reading some passage in the classics, he " translate it aloud and continuously into English prose." Lord Mahon says that the favorite author of Pitt in his youth was Demosthenes.[29] Unfortunately we have none of the speeches of the elder Pitt in the form in which they were delivered. Some single passages and one speech said to have been revised by him are all on which we can depend for our own estimate of the characteristics of his oratory. But these fragments confirm the testimony of his contemporaries that in almost every quality of eloquence his speeches were of the Demosthenic type. Men who heard him, tell of his rapid vehemence, his intense feeling, his terrible invective, his variety and unexpectedness, the impression of sincerity which he gives, and, above all, the moral elevation of his ideas. Lord Brougham says of him: " More than any other orator since

Demosthenes, he was distinguished by the grandeur of feeling with which he regarded, and the amplitude of survey which he cast upon the subject-matters of debate." Now this enumeration of qualities might well have been written as a description of the oratory of Demosthenes — there would be little to alter if that had been its purpose. But were these qualities the result of the study of the Greek orator? Probably there was no conscious imitation, but in view of the devotion of the young man to rhetorical training and his partiality for the speeches of Demosthenes, it is not too much to conclude that in the formative period of his education and by his later studies, his own style was very definitely influenced by that of the Greek master.

The oratory of Edmund Burke in its matured form is distinctly Ciceronian, rather than Demosthenic. We have not sufficient knowledge of his early studies to determine to what extent he was familiar with Demosthenes in the original. Sir Philip Francis is authority for the statement that " Cicero was the model on which he labored to form his own character, in eloquence, in policy, in ethics and philosophy." Yet his natural exuberance of fancy and his impatience of restraint needed the discipline of Demosthenic speech rather than the example of the Ciceronian rhetoric.

The speeches of Fox were so entirely extemporaneous, so unstudied in form and expression, that any influence which the style of Demosthenes may have had upon his own must have been due chiefly to the shaping of his standards during his school and university studies, when he was a diligent student of Greek. Lord Brougham [30] sees his only real resemblance to Demosthenes in the fact that " his eloquence was fervid, rapid, copious, carrying along with it the minds of the audience, nor suffering them to dwell upon the speaker or the speech, but engrossing their whole attention, and keeping it fixed on the question."

If one could combine the condensed reasoning of Thucydides with the clearness and force of Demosthenes, his style would be very like that of the younger Pitt: — sentences usually short and simple, yet forcible; in culminating passages, periods of greater length and real power; no ornament for ornament's sake, no longdrawn and flowery similes, like those of Burke; appeal to emotion, but resting on the conviction of reason. We know that at Cambridge Pitt was trained especially in Thucydides; it is a safe assumption that in his well-attested command of the Greek classics, Demosthenes was not neglected.

Henry Grattan, well grounded in the classics at Trinity College, Dublin, devoted himself to training in oratory in the course of his law-studies in London. It was his practice to copy and declaim passages from Bolingbroke and Chatham, and from the Greek and Roman orators. Henry Flood, his early associate in the fight for Irish liberties, had translated some of the speeches of Demosthenes, and we hear of his reading them to Grattan and a little group of friends. Grattan himself, writing to his son, urges him not to forget " to read out loud every day some portion of Homer, Milton, and Demosthenes." Not only did Grattan find in Demosthenes inspiration for his own struggle for the liberties of his country, but his speeches show everywhere the effect of the Demosthenic style. We should expect that Grattan's Irish emotions would carry him over to the Ciceronian exuberance, and that his oratory would be like that of Burke; but on the contrary there is everywhere a fine, almost Attic, restraint; only in the strongest and culminating attacks do we find him throwing off restraint, and there, indeed, he has Demosthenes for a model. He is intense, rapid; his clear, usually short, sentences are intensified by antithesis and verbal emphasis; his occasional longer periods have climactic power — very rarely do they pass beyond the Greek standard of length; his invective would rejoice the heart of his Greek master; he outdoes the Greek in the use of sententious epigrams, "profound, sagacious, and original." [31] Twice we find in Grattan clear reminiscences of the *Crown Speech*. He closes an enumeration of the oppressive acts of the Council with the words, " The day would expire before I could recount their ill-doings." So Demosthenes said (§ 296): " The day will fail me recounting the names of the traitors." In Grattan's attack on Mr. Corry there is a parody on the following words of Demosthenes (§ 242): " A base thing, fellow citizens, a base thing is the slanderer and from every point of view abusive and malignant; but this little apology for a man is a puppy by nature; nothing sound nor free has he ever done; an arrant tragic ape, a rustic Oenomaus, a counterfeit statesman." Of Mr. Corry, Grattan says: " Am I to renounce these habits now forever, and at the

beck of whom? I should rather say, of what —
half a minister and half a monkey — a 'prentice
politician, and a master coxcomb."

George Canning was known at Eton as one
of the most brilliant classical scholars. We have
no testimony as to his studies in Demosthenes,
but in one of his early speeches he shows his
familiarity with him by an extended free para-
phrase of a passage of fifteen lines from the
speech *On the Chersonese*. Here Canning ap-
plies to the menace from Napoleon's power the
warnings of Demosthenes against that of
Philip.[32] Canning's political principles were
not such as to make him sympathetic toward
Demosthenes' enthusiasm for democracy. Devoted to the Tory cause, the enemy of all
radical movements for reform, Canning could
follow Demosthenes only in his enthusiasm for
national independence and power. Canning's
style has nothing of the Attic simplicity and restraint. The early speeches suffer through their
long and rather involved sentences; the later
ones have attained clearness, and show infinite
ingenuity in argumentation, but there is little
of beauty or of the Demosthenic sharpness of
expression and depth of emotion. When Canning attempts oratorical flights, he amplifies

[161]

and expands till his page-long periods break apart of their own weight.

Lord Brougham (1778–1868), although in his studies at Edinburgh more interested in mathematics and natural science, brought to his professional career a love for Greek and Roman oratory which not only had a very marked influence on his style in public speech, but made him during his parliamentary career an enthusiastic student of Demosthenes, and after his middle life a translator and interpreter of two of his speeches. Always the champion of freedom and reform, the enemy of the slave-trade and of Catholic disabilities, and of the rotten-borough system of parliamentary representation, Brougham found in Demosthenes' struggles for liberty and democracy ideals which appealed to him utterly. In his speeches he twice made effective use of quotations from Demosthenes.[33] Brougham's style, wherever it passes beyond the informal, argumentative type of the ordinary English statesman, as it always does in his perorations, and not infrequently in the body of the speech, shows the influence of his studies in Demosthenes. He has good command of the short, sharp period of two parallel or antithetic cola; he makes very frequent use of the *sensus suspensio,* only occasionally allowing himself to over-amplify and expand, as Canning and most of the other parliamentarians so generally do. His Greek studies have protected him from the Ciceronian exuberance and ornamentation which are always lying in wait for Burke's highest attempts at eloquence. Brougham was perhaps as nearly Demosthenic as it was possible for a member of the English Parliament in his time to become.

Lord Wellesley, parliamentarian in Ireland and England, and able administrator in India, offers one of the finest examples of the enthusiastic pursuit of studies in classical oratory continued throughout an active political career. Lord Brougham tells us [34] that Wellesley's earlier Demosthenic studies had been confined to the speeches *On the Embassy* and *On the Crown,* and that he knew the latter ' by heart,' but that long studies and discussion with Brougham himself brought him finally to the recognition of " the extraordinary beauties of the *Philippics*." Brougham tells us however that the chief influence of Demosthenes on Wellesley's own oratory was in keeping him from " all tinsel and vulgar ornaments," for in other respects his style — diffuse and redundant in

[163]

phraseology — was modelled rather on that of Cicero.

The American colleges of the eighteenth century, basing their curricula on those of the English schools and universities, gave a large place to classical studies, but students came to them with little preparation in Greek as compared with that offered by the great English preparatory schools. The American college boys read something of Demosthenes, if only so much as was included in *Graeca Majora,* the standard book of extracts from Greek authors. The spirit and tone of Demosthenes they could appreciate, but probably only a few had sufficient command of the Greek language to permit his style to have much influence on their own. It was only those men who carried the study of Greek oratory beyond their college years who were likely to appreciate the refinements of his style. But in the early nineteenth century we hear of a most interesting senior course at Yale College, in which from about 1822 onward Professor Chauncey A. Goodrich made the study of the speech of Demosthenes *On the Crown* " the basis of a course of informal lectures on the principles of oratory." [35]

The chair of rhetoric as a distinct department at Harvard was first filled by John Quincy Adams, who lectured from 1806 to 1809 in intervals between his services at Washington as Senator from Massachusetts. These lectures, published in 1810, are based chiefly on Cicero and Quintilian, but they show appreciative acquaintance with Demosthenes. Adams quotes a long passage from Demosthenes *On Organization* (XIII) and compares it with a passage from Burke; he quotes a ' transition ' passage from the *Crown Speech,* and makes good use of it; in his discussion of periodic structure he uses a strong antithetic period of the *First Olynthiac,* and under ' Figures ' he quotes the Marathonian oath, saying of it: " This is perhaps the most admired stroke of eloquence that ever was uttered by this first of human orators. It exhibits a grandeur and generosity of sentiment to which the heart of every virtuous man, through all the lapse of ages, must yield assent." In the diary of his ambassadorship at St. Petersburg he says he has been reading the *Fourth Philippic,* and he discusses the problem of composition involved in it. He closes the entry of Dec. 21, 1811 with these words: " The Athenians were not altogether blameless in their proceedings towards Philip. But their faults were all of petty extent, and in the nature of defence. Philip's wrong was enormous; it was the design of subjugating to himself all Greece. He winds his web round them like a spider round a fly. When I read those noble sentiments of Demosthenes in which he compares the fortune of Athens with that of Philip, and prefers it upon the principle that truth and justice *must* be favored by Heaven; when he contends that success and prosperity founded on fraud and treachery *must* be short-lived, I cannot avoid a feeling of sorrow that these maxims were not sanctioned by the event — that the triumph of fraud and treachery was complete, and that liberty sunk under the genius and industry of the tyrant. I remark, as an item in estimating the oratorical power of Demosthenes, that there is nothing like learning in these orations. There is nothing that discovers a cultivated mind. There is little of philosophy, no indulgence to the imagination, no wit or humor, no attempt at ridicule; he is sufficiently figurative, but all his figures are taken from familiar objects. His eloquence is characteristic of democracy, as that of Cicero is of aristocracy. It is the Doric to the Corinthian pillar." These comments show a real appreciation of the spirit of Demosthenes, however inadequate the criticism of his style may be. A study of the speeches of John Quincy Adams will show that his studies in Demosthenes had small effect on his own style. Evidently Cicero and Burke were his models. His inaugural address on taking the chair of rhetoric at Harvard is ornate and artificial — it shows nothing of Attic simplicity and force. His matured eloquence reveals, indeed, a considerable ability to state things clearly and forcibly, but whenever he tries to become eloquent he passes over into the current flowery and high-flown style; even his vocabulary is stilted and unnatural.

Rufus Choate, second only to Webster among American orators, was not only a brilliant classical scholar during his course at Dartmouth, but perhaps more than any other American in public life he carried the study of Greek and Latin throughout his professional career. In his busiest years he found time every day for the reading of classical authors.[36] While, according to Choate, Cicero and Burke are the models for the young student of eloquence and should be known ' by heart,' he gives large place to Greek prose and poetry. Under date of De-

cember 9, 1844 he enters in his journal the
resolution to add to the " *Odyssey,* Thucydides,
Tacitus, Juvenal, and some French orator or
critic," together with " Milton, Johnson, Burke
— *semper in manu* " — the study of Demosthenes *On the Crown*, "which I will completely
master, translate, annotate, and commit." He
soon added Thucydides. Writing on the thirtieth
of May, 1845, he says: " Translation daily is
manifestly my only means of keeping up my
English. This I practise in my post-prandial
readings, but I fear it is not quite exacting,
laborious, and stimulant enough. I have a pretty
strong impression that the only sufficient task
would be Demosthenes severely, exactly ren-
dered, yet with utmost striving of words, style,
melody, volume of sound, and impression. I
should begin with the oration *For the Crown*."
This was written in the midst of Choate's duties
at Washington in his last session of Congress.
The fruits of these Demosthenic studies are
gathered together in Choate's oration, *The
Eloquence of Revolutionary Periods*, delivered
two years before his death. Here the significance
of Demosthenes' statesmanship and the power
of his oratory are summed up with an insight
into the issues of the Athenian struggle and the

elements of Demosthenes' power as an orator which rivals the best that Lord Brougham has written, and has no superior in the discussions by our later historians and critics. And here, too, we can trace something of the effect of his Greek studies on Choate's own style. There is little of the former stilted vocabulary, the words are simple and natural; the sentences are for the most part simple and clear. When the thought is cast in the periodic form, it is usually without undue amplification. If in some parts the style is more Ciceronian than Demosthenic, it is certainly free from the bombast and artificiality of his predecessors.

A contemporary of Choate's, Hugh Swinton Legaré of South Carolina, lawyer and publicist, was an equally enthusiastic student of Demosthenes. Choate considered Legaré's essay *Demosthenes, the Man, the Statesman, and the Orator*, superior to Lord Brougham's treatise. It certainly shows a wide and minute acquaintance with Demosthenes' speeches, and a statesmanlike understanding of the public issues involved in them.[87] Legaré's own style in the few speeches which we have, shows a clearness and restraint of expression not usual in the speeches of his time. His study of Greek oratory, if it did not make him eloquent, did protect him from the current abuses of the rhetorical manner.

Edward Everett, whose career began with the professorship of Greek at Harvard, was throughout a long life our finest representative of epideictic oratory. In the eulogy and the panegyric address he brought all the resources of the Greek rhetoric to the service of American history. His repeated references to Demosthenes attest his admiration of his oratory; but Everett was by disposition and by circumstance kept apart from violent discussion until the crisis of the Civil War recalled him from the retirement of old age to inspire and hearten his fellow-citizens. Here at last we find something of Demosthenic fervor, but the life-long rhetorical habit colors even these patriotic appeals. In the best of Everett's orations we have a type intermediate between the ornate and loosely composed periodic structure of the earlier American oratory and the matter-of-fact style of our own time. His service to the development of a dignified and beautiful prose style was very great, and unquestionably his studies in Greek oratory contributed to this effect.

The American orator who in vehemence of

attack and bitterness of denunciation most resembles Demosthenes is Wendell Phillips, the anti-slavery agitator — the man who called Edward Everett " cuckoo," and Webster " weathercock." His biting sarcasm and ugly epithets might well have been learned in the school of Demosthenes, but it is doubtful whether Phillips had much knowledge of the Greek orator beyond that which any graduate of Harvard in his time would bring from his college studies. On one occasion he does show that he knows the speeches *On the Crown;* President Felton, eulogizing Daniel Webster, had made use of Demosthenes' speech; Phillips retorts with a telling passage from the speech of Aeschines.[38]

Daniel Webster's oratory was the product of his own genius. His native reasoning power was brightened by poetic inspiration and deep emotion. His style was modelled on that of the British orators and of Cicero, but happily simplified by long practice before juries. He probably had only the college boy's knowledge of the Greek of Demosthenes. Sometimes his exuberant imagination carried him over to the ornate style of Burke. A better acquaintance with Demosthenes might have protected him here, as it

did Rufus Choate. Indeed, in later life Webster expressed regret at his inability to read
and understand Demosthenes in the original.[39]
Shortly after the death of Daniel Webster, his
intimate friend, Professor Felton, later President of Harvard, contributed to the *American
Whig Review* (Dec. 1852) an extended appreciation of Webster as statesman and orator. He
closes with a long and striking parallel between
the public services and oratory of Webster and
of Demosthenes.

As we review the course of British oratory
down to the middle of the nineteenth century
we find Cicero to have been the dominant influence, perhaps in part because most university
men, even in England, went out from their
academic studies with a more familiar knowledge of Latin than of Greek, in part also
because Attic oratory in its restraint and simplicity needs an Attic mind for its full appreciation. Doubtless the universal study of the
rhetoric of Cicero and Quintilian tended also to
fix the Ciceronian type upon English oratory.
Yet the oratory of Demosthenes was a very real
influence, not only in inspiring democratic and

patriotic principles, but in shaping the style of some of the ablest men in public life.

In America the English orators were naturally the models, and their Ciceronianism was considerably reinforced by the study of Cicero himself, and by the very general study of rhetoric, with all its adornments and ' figures.' It was only in exceptional cases that the study of Demosthenes was carried far enough to have any considerable influence on style; his thought and the principles of his public life were always and everywhere appreciated and admired.

English and American oratory since the middle of the nineteenth century has been less affected by classical models. The simplicity of style in all prose writing and the contempt for everything ' rhetorical ' have greatly improved public speaking. But here there is serious danger lest with the elimination of the artificial ornaments of oratory we lose the essential elements of force and of the appeal to the emotions. A speech is not an essay, and it has its own laws of power and effectiveness. No greater service could be done toward the recovery of the influence of the spoken word both in England and America than by a revival of the study of the Greek masterpieces. The relegation of the study of Demosthenes to the closets of classical philology has been a disaster to the cause of effective oratory.

NOTES AND BIBLIOGRAPHY

NOTES

1. The author has made his own translations of Demosthenes for this volume, but doubtless many expressions borrowed from English translators and commentators have been so long used by him in his classes as to seem to him his own.

2. The author has discussed this affair at length in " The Harpalos Case," in *Transactions of the American Philological Association*, XXXII. 121–153 (1901).

3. We have an able and elaborate study of the plan of the *Crown Speech* in the volume of Wilhelm Fox, *Die Kranzrede des Demosthenes*, Leipzig, 1880.

4. We owe the recognition of this piece of strategy to Henri Weil, who called attention to it in a paper "Sur le Discours de la Couronne," (Annuaire de l'assoc. p. l'encouragement des études grecq, pp. 170–184, Paris, 1876). It has not received the attention which it deserves; it is fundamental to an understanding of the strategy of the speech.

5. Lord Brougham, *Dissertation on the Eloquence of the Ancients*, pp. 48 ff.

6. Cf. *Aeschines Against Ctesiphon*, §§ 132 ff., §§ 157 ff.

7. The proper technical term for the elements of a 'period' is 'kola'; the 'clause' is an element of a logical unit, the sentence; a 'kolon' is an element of a rhetorical unit, the period. Sentence and period oftentimes do not coincide. Frequently only a small portion of a sentence forms a period, sometimes several periods are embedded in a single sentence. For a more extended discussion of periodic structure, with illustrations of the several types, see the author's *Lysias, Selected Speeches*, New York, 1905, pp. 345–352.

8. We find a striking period of this type in *De Cor.*, § 71:

When Philip was appropriating Euboea
and preparing it as a rampart over against Attica,
and making his attempts on Megara
and seizing Oreus
and ravaging Porthmus,
and in Oreus setting up Philistides as tyrant
and in Eretria Kleitarchus,
and bringing the Hellespont under his own power
and besieging Byzantium,
and overturning some Greek states
and into others bringing back their exiles,
IN DOING ALL THIS WAS HE DOING WRONG AND BREAKING
  HIS AGREEMENTS
AND VIOLATING THE PEACE, OR NOT?
AND WAS IT TIME FOR SOME ONE OF THE GREEK STATES
  TO STAND FORTH TO HINDER, OR NOT?

The climax of such a period of *sensus suspensio* is often followed by one or more kola which reinforce and intensify the final thought. (Cf. *De Cor.*, § 199.) Not only are the speeches full of periods based on antithesis, but antithesis of kola is very common within periods based on *sensus suspensio*. (Cf. *De Chers.*, § 69.)

9. Lord Brougham in his *Inaugural Discourse* fully discusses and illustrates this restraint of Demosthenes. A good illustration of Edmund Burke's picturesque amplification is his prediction of the dire results of a policy of forcing the American colonists to pass over into the immense plain, " a square of five hundred miles," west of the Appalachians: " Over this they would wander without a possibility of restraint. They would change their manners with the habits of their life; would soon forget a government by which they were disowned; would become hordes of English Tartars and, pouring down upon your unfortified frontiers a fierce and irresistible cavalry, become masters of your governors and your counselors, your collectors and controllers, and of all the slaves that adhered to them." (*On Conciliation with America*)

10. Cf. also *De Chers.*, § 22; *Olynth.*, II. § 27; *Embassy*, §§ 275, 289.

11. Eduard Norden, *Die Antike Kunstprosa*, Leipzig, 1898, pp. 788 ff., traces the artificial style of Lyly to the influence of Gorgias himself, through the intermediary work of the Spaniard Guevara, whose *Marcus Aurelius* (1529) appeared in an English translation by Thomas North in 1568, eleven years before the publication of *Euphues* by Lyly.

12. On the avoidance of short syllables, see the statistics in the author's article, " Demosthenes' Avoidance of *Breves*," in *Classical Philology*, XII. 271-294 (1917).

13. The most promising approach to a solution of the problem of Demosthenic rhythm is in a paper by C. W. E. Miller, " The Pronunciation of Greek and Latin Prose," in *Transactions of the American Philological Association*, LIII. 169-197 (1922).

14. See Engelbert Drerup, *Antike Demosthenesausgaben*, Leipzig, 1899.

15. Only the introduction has been preserved. Some critics doubt whether the translation itself was ever completed.

16. We have this work in an admirable edition, with English translation, by W. Rhys Roberts, *Longinus on the Sublime*,[2] Cambridge, England, 1907. Roberts gives at length the reasons which have led most recent scholars to place this work in the first century A.D., rejecting the traditional ascription to Longinus of the third century. Quotations in the text are from Roberts' translation.

17. W. Rhys Roberts has edited this treatise also, with English translation: *Demetrius on Style*, Cambridge, England, 1902. He discusses the question of date and authorship, at length.

18. Other writers of the same period who comment on Demosthenes and quote from him are: Theon, an Alexandrian teacher; *Anonymus Seguerius*, in Leonard Spengel, *Rhetores Graeci*, Leipzig, I. pp. 352 ff. (Hammer, Ed., 1894); Alexander, son of Numenius, rhetorician; Rufus of Perinthus; Polemon, who is said to have set up a bust of Demosthenes at Pergamum, a city in which rhetorical studies were especially cultivated.

19. For the text and a detailed discussion of the *Demosthenis Laudatio,* see the edition of F. Albers, Leipzig, 1910. Cf. Engelbert Drerup, *Demosthenes im Urteile des Altertums,* Würzburg, 1923, pp. 151 ff.

20. Hermogenes in the *Rhetoric* quotes Demosthenes 337 times, Isocrates 10 times, Aeschines 8; he has no quotations from Lysias, Hyperides, or Isaeus.

21. For comments on other writers on rhetoric and oratory, such as Apsines of Gadara, Tiberius, Minucianus, see Drerup, *op. cit.,* pp. 148 ff. Imaginary declamations on historical subjects were favorite exercises in the schools of rhetoric. Among those which have come down to us, subjects taken from the career of Demosthenes have a large place.

22. W. Schmid, " Die sogenannte Aristidesrhetorik," in *Rheinisches Museum,* LXXII. 113, 238 (1917–18), shows how such rhetorical commentaries on Demosthenes for school use lie back of the first part of a *Rhetoric* ascribed to Aristides, and of the *Rhetoric* of Hermogenes. They abandoned the old classification of prose writing as in three styles, the ' grand,' the ' plain,' and the ' intermediate,' substituting for these the numerous features (ἰδέαι) of good prose, such as dignity, severity, purity, sweetness, conciseness, clearness, etc. Political oratory reaches its perfection in Demosthenes, and his supreme characteristic is " mastery " (δεινότης). Unfortunately none of these rhetorical Demosthenes school-commentaries have survived.

23. For the latest discussion of the sources of these " Lives," see Drerup, *op. cit.,* pp. 129 ff.

24. See Drerup, *op. cit.,* p. 147.

25. On the work of Chrysoloras and Vittorino, see W. H. Woodward, *Vittorino da Feltre and Other Humanist Educators,* Cambridge, England, 1897.

26. Reiske's edition contained the whole corpus; Taylor's, only about half of the speeches.

27. For a review of Meyer and Wendland, who exalted the political program of Isocrates as against that of Demosthenes, see the author's article, " Recent Views of the Political Influence of Isocrates," in *Classical Philology,* VII. 343–350 (1912).

28. Cf. Drerup's quotation (p. 2) from the *Kölnische Zeitung* of Jan. 31, 1916: " Nein! Dieser Krieg gilt nicht der Demokratie, sondern der Vorherrschaft des regierenden Advokatenstandes in England und Frankreich, die sich zu einem der grössten Kulturschäden ausgewachsen hat." In his later volume, *Demosthenes im Urteile des Altertums,* Würzburg, 1923, Drerup is equally outspoken in expressing his opinion of democracy in the New Germany: " Denn auch in unserm einst so stolzen Vaterlande herrscht heute eine Republik der Gasse und der Demagogen, deren sich ein Kleon und der Wursthändler des Aristophanes nicht zu schämen brauchten " (p. 1).

Clemenceau's *Démosthène* was published in Paris, 1926. An English translation by C. M. Thompson followed (Boston, 1926).

29. Perhaps Thucydides should be added, for we know that in directing the university studies of his son, Chatham gave first place to the reading of Thucydides and Polybius, and that he himself helped Smith, the translator of Thucydides, in the revision of one of the speeches of Pericles.

30. Henry, Lord Brougham, *Historical Sketches of Statesmen Who Flourished in the Time of George III,* 2 vols., Philadelphia, 1840; I. p. 155.

31. For an appreciative summary of the excellencies of Grattan's oratory, see W. E. H. Lecky, *The Leaders of Public Opinion in Ireland,* London and New York, 1872, pp. 108 ff.

32. George Canning, *Respecting Peace with France,* Dec. 11, 1798, *Speeches,* Vol. I. p. 117; Demosthenes, *On the Chersonese,* §§ 49 ff.

33. In the peroration of the speech *On the Slave Trade,* 1838, *Speeches,* Vol. II, p. 178, Brougham cites in the Greek the splendid passage, οὐ λίθοις ἐτείχισα τὴν πόλιν (*De Corona,* § 299). In the defence of Queen Caroline (*Speeches,* Vol. I. p. 212) he quotes Demosthenes on 'Distrust' (ἀπιστία), as Nature's safeguard for the weak against the strong (*Phil.,* II. 24).

34. *Statesmen in the Time of George III,* (Third Series), pp. 270 ff.

35. See the preface of C. A. Goodrich, *Select British Eloquence*, New York, 1852.

36. The source of this account of Choate's classical studies is his own *Journal*, as given in S. G. Brown's *Works of Rufus Choate*, 2 vols., Boston, 1862; vol. I.

37. Legaré's essay was published in the *New York Review*, July 1841, and was reprinted in Vol. I. of his collected works, *Writings of Hugh S. Legaré*, 2 vols., Philadelphia, 1846. It deserves the careful attention of students of Greek oratory. Few Americans in public life at any period could have written such an essay.

38. Wendell Phillips' lecture, *Idols; Aeschines against Ctesiphon*, §§ 245 ff.

39. "After leaving college, I 'caught up,' as the boys say, pretty well in Latin; but in college and afterwards I left Greek to Loveland, and mathematics to Shattuck. Would that I had pursued Greek till I could read and understand Demosthenes in his own language!" Letter of Webster to his classmate Merrill. *Writings and Speeches of Daniel Webster*, Boston, 1903; XVIII. pp. 411 ff.

BIBLIOGRAPHY

BLASS, FRIEDRICH, *Die Attische Beredsamkeit*, III, i, *Demosthenes.*[2] Leipzig, 1893.

BROUGHAM, HENRY, LORD, *Dissertation on the Eloquence of the Ancients; Inaugural Discourse; Demosthenes,* in Brougham's *Works,* Vol. VII. Edinburgh, 1872.

BRUNS, IVO, *Das literarische Porträt der Griechen.* Berlin, 1896.

BUTCHER, S. H., *Demosthenes,* in *Classical Writers* series. London, 1893.

BUTCHER RENNIE, *Demosthenis Orationes,* I, II Pt. i., BUTCHER, S. H.; II Pt. ii, Rennie, W. Oxford, 1903–1920.

PICKARD-CAMBRIDGE, A. W., *Demosthenes and the Last Days of Greek Freedom,* in *Heroes of the Nations* series. New York and London, 1914.

CHOATE, RUFUS, *The Eloquence of Revolutionary Periods,* in *Works,* Vol. I. Boston, 1862.

CROISET, A. ET M., *Histoire de la Littérature Grecque.* 5 vols. Paris, 1887–1899; vol. 4, Chapter 8, Démosthène.

DOBSON, J. F., *The Greek Orators.* London, 1919.

DRERUP, ENGELBERT, *Demosthenes im Urteile des Altertums.* Würzburg, 1923.

FERGUSON, W. S., *Hellenistic Athens.* London and New York, 1911.

GOODWIN, W. W., *Demosthenes on the Crown.* Cambridge, England, 1901.

HOGARTH, D. G., *Philip and Alexander of Macedon.* London and New York, 1897.

HUMPHREYS, M. W., *Demosthenes on the Crown.* New York, 1913.

JEBB, R. C., *The Attic Orators.* 2 vols. London and New York, 1876.

[183]

BIBLIOGRAPHY

NORDEN, EDUARD, *Die Antike Kunstprosa.* 2 vols. Leipzig, 1898.

SCHAEFER, ARNOLD, *Demosthenes und seine Zeit.* 3 vols. Leipzig, 1856–1858. (Revised by Hoffmann, Leipzig, 1885–1887.)

ENGLISH TRANSLATIONS

BROUGHAM, HENRY, LORD, *The Oration of Demosthenes upon the Crown,* in Rutledge's *Sir John Lubbock's Hundred Books.* London, 1893.

——, *The Chersonese Oration,* in *Works,* Vol. VII. Edinburgh, 1872.

PICKARD-CAMBRIDGE, A. W., *The Public Orations of Demosthenes.* 2 vols. Oxford, 1912.

KENNEDY, CHARLES RANN, *The Orations of Demosthenes,* in *Bohn's Classical Library.* 6 vols. London, 1852–1870.

VINCE, C. A. and VINCE, J. H., *Demosthenes, De Corona and De Falsa Legatione,* in *The Loeb Classical Library.* London and New York, 1926.

Our Debt to Greece and Rome

AUTHORS AND TITLES

AUTHORS AND TITLES

AESCHYLUS AND SOPHOCLES. *J. T. Sheppard.*

GREEK RELIGION. *Walter Woodburn Hyde.*

SURVIVALS OF ROMAN RELIGION. *Gordon J. Laing.*

MYTHOLOGY. *Jane Ellen Harrison.*

ANCIENT BELIEFS IN THE IMMORTALITY OF THE SOUL. *Clifford H. Moore.*

STAGE ANTIQUITIES. *James Turney Allen.*

PLAUTUS AND TERENCE. *Gilbert Norwood.*

ROMAN POLITICS. *Frank Frost Abbott.*

PSYCHOLOGY, ANCIENT AND MODERN. *G. S. Brett.*

ANCIENT AND MODERN ROME. *Rodolfo Lanciani.*

WARFARE BY LAND AND SEA. *Eugene S. Mc-Cartney.*

THE GREEK FATHERS. *James Marshall Campbell.*

GREEK BIOLOGY AND MEDICINE. *Henry Osborn Taylor.*

MATHEMATICS. *David Eugene Smith.*

LOVE OF NATURE AMONG THE GREEKS AND ROMANS. *H. R. Fairclough.*

ANCIENT WRITING AND ITS INFLUENCE. *B. L. Ullman.*

GREEK ART. *Arthur Fairbanks.*

ARCHITECTURE. *Alfred M. Brooks.*

ENGINEERING. *Alexander P. Gest.*

MODERN TRAITS IN OLD GREEK LIFE. *Charles Burton Gulick.*

ROMAN PRIVATE LIFE. *Walton Brooks McDaniel.*

GREEK AND ROMAN FOLKLORE. *William Reginald Halliday.*

ANCIENT EDUCATION. *J. F. Dobson.*